Diana

A Tribute to the People's Princess

A Tribute to
the People's Princess

Peter Donnelly

COURAGE
B O O K S
AN IMPRINT OF RUNNING PRESS
PHILADELPHIA • LONDON

Credits

For Quadrillion:

The editorial team: Will Steeds, Chris Stone, Bron Kowal, Phil de Ste. Croix, Jane Alexander
The design team: Sue Mims, Sarah Newby, Teddy Hartshorn
Nicky Chapman, Justina Leitão, Chris Dymond
Production: Gerald Hughes (Production Director), Ruth Arthur, Karen Staff
Colour reproduction: Square Precision Graphics, London

For Bookman Projects: Nick Kent, Hugh Gallacher

Author

PETER DONNELLY, born in County Durham, UK, in 1941, is a widely admired author, biographer and journalist. He has known and written about many famous figures, but has been most highly praised for his book *Mrs. Milburn's Diaries,* the moving story of an ordinary woman who lived through the war years in Coventry. Peter is responsible, along with Nigel Dempster, for the creation of the *Daily Mail Diary*.

Publisher's acknowledgements

The Publishers would particularly like to thank the following people for their help on this project: Nick Kent at Bookman Projects Ltd. for his advice and help throughout the project; James Whitaker of *The Mirror* for his unselfish assistance; Hugh Gallacher for specialist picture research; Alison Hynds for consultancy and picture editing; Jill Palmer, Gill Swain, Lucy Turner, Jan Disley, Ollie Picton-Jones for invaluable editorial contributions; Ric Papineau, of the Academy of Excellence, for his good offices; everyone in Mirror Group's IT department for their help and advice.

Library of Congress Cataloging-in-Publication Number 97-75322
ISBN 0-7624-0326-8

This book was produced by CLB International, Godalming, Surrey, U.K.
in cooperation with Bookman Projects Ltd.

Published by Courage Books, an imprint of
Running Press Book Publishers
125 South Twenty-second Street
Philadelphia, Pennsylvania 19103-4399

Contents

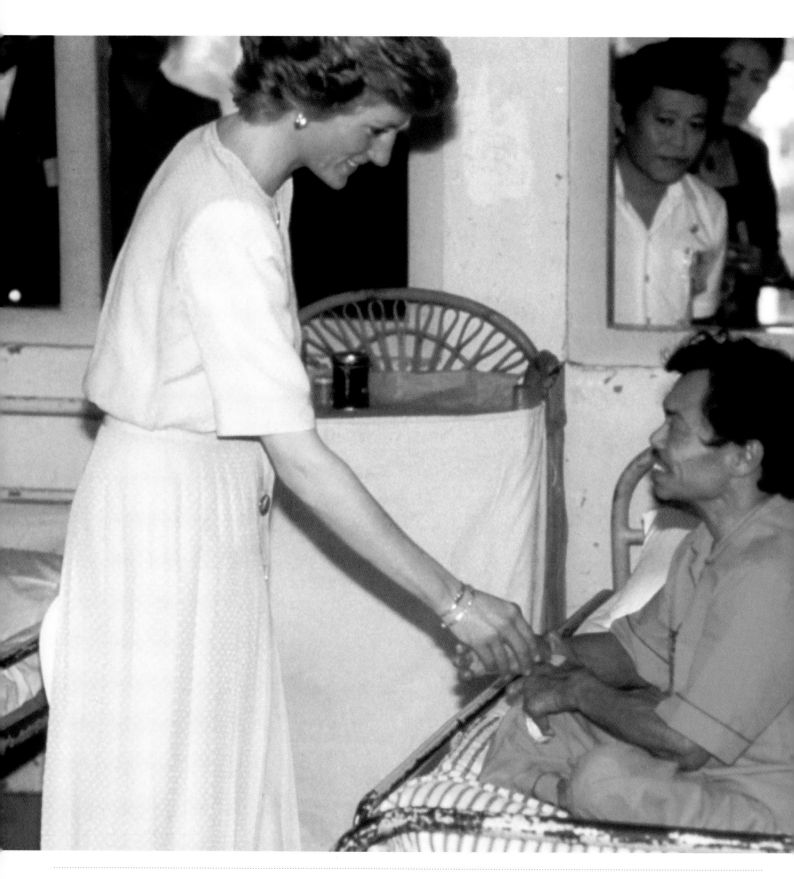

Foreword

I am delighted to have been asked to write the Foreword to *Diana: A Tribute to the People's Princess*. She became Patron of The Leprosy Mission in 1990, after visiting a leprosy hospital despite adverse advice and criticism. Leprosy may not only be mentally and physically damaging, but it is often erroneously seen as a curse from the gods, and the 'victims' then become outcasts. Since Diana herself was the frequent victim of pain and anguish, she had a special empathy for those who suffered in the same way. It is not a coincidence that five of her six remaining charities are associated with stigma.

She was charismatic, witty and, above all, a woman of extraordinary compassion. This was demonstrated both in the limelight and, more often, when there were no cameras or reporters present. On one occasion in Harare she was touring a hospital ward run by The Leprosy Mission when she saw a patient with badly deformed hands using a sewing machine to make a dress. She asked me about the lady sewing and a ward nurse replied, 'She came in a leper and is going out a person; a Christian seamstress'. Instead of proceeding along the ward as expected, the Princess disappeared behind a partition. She was in tears. It was not because she felt sorry for the lady, but rather she was so overwhelmed by the recovered hope and dignity which the lady now possessed.

She was a huge force for good, now gone from the world. Her power lay not in political status but in the wealth of her overwhelming compassion for those in need. I am grateful that this book will, in some way, help perpetuate her work and her memory.

Tony Lloyd

The Reverend Tony Lloyd,
Executive Director,
The Leprosy Mission,
Peterborough PE2 5GZ, UK

"Diana was very fond of pretty clothes and kept them neat. She loved floral dresses and used to go shopping with her mother for party outfits…She wasn't easy. Some children that young will do as they are told immediately, but Diana wouldn't, it was always a battle of wills. She was full of spirit. But she was a lovely child, and after she had been reasoned with she would usually co-operate — eventually."

The Making of a Princess

Lessons in life for a young lady

She always knew she was set apart somehow, and once said as much, without sounding in the least pompous: 'I was always detached from everyone else. I knew I was going somewhere different, that I was in the wrong shell.'

That 'somewhere different' was a privileged place as an icon of her age, a woman instantly recognised in every corner of the globe, a glamorous but still very accessible cover-girl hailed as 'the People's Princess' and finally, through her compassion and concern for others and her absolute commitment to them, as the 'Queen of People's Hearts', a role she craved above all others.

There was an initial public misconception that Diana Spencer, the first Englishwoman to marry an heir to the throne for more than 300 years, was in fact 'just an ordinary girl'. Far from it: the Honourable Diana Frances Spencer was born at Park House, on the Queen's Sandringham estate in Norfolk, late in the afternoon of July 1, 1961.

She was the third daughter of Viscount Althorp, the eighth Earl Spencer, who had been an equerry both to George VI and the Queen. Her maternal grandmother, Ruth, Lady Fermoy, was a close friend and lady in waiting to the Queen Mother. And through these close links with the British royal family, she became a childhood playmate of her future husband's younger brothers, Prince Andrew and Prince Edward.

Hers, though, was a far from happy childhood. When she was just six years old, her mother left her father for the wallpaper heir Peter Shand Kydd, depriving Diana of the full-time mother-love that she came to believe was so vitally important for her own children, and others.

The Viscountess sought custody of her two youngest children, Diana and Charles Althorp,

Top: Park House, Sandringham, where Lady Diana Spencer was born on July 1, 1961.
Above: Early years should be a time of joy for a family, but Diana's childhood was to be overshadowed by growing disharmony between her parents.

but was thwarted by her mother Ruth, who told the court they should remain with their father. The couple were divorced in 1969 and Diana continued to live at Park House until the death of her grandfather, the seventh Earl, in 1975.

The family then moved to the Spencer family seat at Althorp House in Northamptonshire, but this change of home did not signal a happier new stage in Diana's life. She would

> *"I shall only get married when I am sure that I am in love, so that we will never be divorced."*

tiptoe downstairs and, leaning over the banisters, watch as her mother and father bitterly fought out their continuing battles.

But most of the time she hid her face in the bed covers. She developed a fear of the dark and had bad dreams: 'I just couldn't bear it. It was a testing time.'

For Diana, the day her mother packed her bags and left meant a succession of nannies, most of whom described her as 'difficult' or 'tricky'. She told one of them, Mary Clarke: 'I shall only get married when I am sure I am in love, so that we will never be divorced.'

Another nanny, Janet Thompson, who started work with Diana when she was just three years old, recalls: 'She would call out to me to bring her a glass of water or to take her to the loo in the middle of the night. Sometimes she would wake up after a bad dream and would cry. I would have to talk to her gently. Then in the morning she would come into my room and creep into bed with me to keep warm, and for a cuddle.'

Even at that age, Diana had a passion for two things which stayed with her all her life – clothes and sweets. Nanny Janet Thompson remembers:

Above: Diana the tomboy. In fact, even as a young child she was already very fond of pretty dresses and loved shopping for clothes with her mother.

'Diana was very fond of pretty clothes and kept them neat. She loved floral dresses and used to go shopping with her mother for party outfits.

They were a very sociable family, and were out all the time at tea parties, so Diana needed a good choice.' But sometimes her young charge could be a handful: 'She wasn't easy. Some children that young will do as they are told immediately, but Diana wouldn't, it was always a battle of wills. She was full of spirit. But she was a lovely child, and after she had been reasoned with she would usually co-operate – eventually.'

Though she played with the royal children when she was young, Diana never shared their enthusiasm for horses and dogs. Elder sister Sarah was horse mad, but Diana never saw the point of it all. Once, when she was 10, the sisters went riding together. Diana's horse bolted and she was thrown off, breaking her arm.

She was wary of horses from then on, although after her marriage she did try to please the Queen and Prince Philip by trying to learn to ride well, but gave it up as a bad job.

Nanny Thompson's departure coincided with the breakup of the marriage of Viscount Althorp and his wife, a traumatic time for their children. But it was nothing compared to the arrival of the new woman in their father's life – the formidable Raine Spencer, or 'Acid Raine' as they came to call her.

The children so hated Raine – the former Countess of Dartmouth and daughter of the romantic novelist Barbara Cartland – that they composed poison-pen letters to try to drive her away.

If life at home was insecure, Diana's arrival at Sifield School in nearby King's Lynn in 1968 did little to improve matters. She was not as clever as her younger brother and he nicknamed her 'Brian' after the dim-witted snail in the children's TV show *The Magic Roundabout*.

'I longed to be as good as him in the schoolroom,' she recalled. 'I wasn't any good at anything. I felt hopeless, a drop-out. Brain the size of a pea – that's what I've got. I'm as thick as a plank.'

Nor did she do much better at Riddlesworth Hall, the boarding school near Diss in Norfolk to which she was sent when she was nine. In fact Diana would never shine academically – a fact cynics cruelly noted in later years – but she had other qualities which more than adequately compensated for her scholarly deficiencies.

Away from her family, painfully shy and lonely, she felt instant compassion for others suffering the same plight: 'She was awfully

Above: Playtime – nanny Janet Thompson and Diana play Blind Man's Buff while mother Frances holds Charles in her arms. Below: Diana and her younger brother Charles pictured in 1968.

Above: Family portrait. Behind the happy façade, the marriage was under strain.
Left: Family snapshot. Diana, a rather round-faced three-year-old, poses for the camera.

sweet with the little ones,' her former head-teacher recalled. 'She could often be found comforting a tearful child, even though she was little more than a child herself.' Baby brother Charles, now Earl Spencer, also received the Diana mothering treatment.

In time Diana followed family tradition – and her mother and sisters Jane and Sarah – to West Heath, the all-girls public school near Sevenoaks in Kent, where, unsurprisingly to those who knew her, one of the most expensive educations that money can buy failed to help her win a single successful examination result. She failed all her 'O' levels, even at the second taking, and left the school at 16.

But she had done well at sport, especially swimming, netball and tennis, and she started ballet and tap-dancing lessons, which provided a welcome escape: 'It always released the tremendous tension in my head.'

And as West Heath encouraged pupils to visit the old and the sick, Diana found her forte. She spent hours visiting an old lady in a near-

Above: Diana, aged 11, at Sandringham with her pet guinea pig 'Peanuts'. From an early age she revealed an instinctive sympathy with people and animals.

Above: London, 1968. Diana's parents' marriage had broken down during the previous year.

Above (and inset): By her own admission, Diana was not a star at school. 'Brain the size of a pea' was her candid self-assessment. Here she is seen at Riddlesworth Hall boarding school, where she started in 1970.

Above: On the Isle of Uist, a teenage Diana looks somewhat ill at ease in her country casuals
Right: A carefree moment with Shetland pony 'Soufflé' in the summer of 1974 at her mother's estate in Scotland.

by town – and while others were unwilling to visit the local mental hospital, Diana found an instant rapport with the handicapped teenagers.

After a brief stay at the Institut Alpin Videmanette, an expensive Swiss finishing school, her father bought her a small flat in Coleherne Court on the borders of London's Kensington – and the 19-year-old Diana embarked upon what – in later days – she would look back on as one of the happiest periods of her life.

Sharing the flat with three best girlfriends, she was at last free to do as she pleased. On three days a week, she worked for well-heeled friends, cleaning floors for £1 an hour, serving canapes at cocktail parties and acting as nanny. Then she took a job for which she was ideally suited, as an assistant working with young children at the Young England kindergarten in Pimlico.

Very soon now she would become public property – her life would never be the same again for the eyes of the world were to be turned upon her. But for now she spent happy, giggling days with her friends, enjoying life to the full.

Left: Even as a young teenager, Diana displayed a natural poise in front of the camera, tempered by a hint of diffidence. This girl would become one of the most photographed women in the world.

The girl who clicked with the camera

It wasn't long before the young Diana was spotted by one of Britain's most experienced royal-watchers – James Whitaker of *The Mirror*. He recalls 'I first set eyes on her in January, 1978. I was captivated'.

Whitaker noticed the attractive 16-year-old standing next to Prince Charles while he was out shooting pheasants with seven other guns at Sandringham:

'She was peering at me and a photographer colleague down a long, tree-lined path through a pair of powerful binoculars', he says. 'But as they were still attached by a strap to Charles' neck, his head was at a funny angle!'

'They were both laughing uproariously, and very clearly happy. But I was mystified why it was Diana standing with Charles and not her sister, Lady Sarah, who was his girlfriend at the time and was also at Sandringham. My immediate thought was that she was there "for Prince Andrew".'

But by July 1980, just a few months before the 'Romance of the Century' began, Diana was spotted again and again wherever Charles happened to be – at a polo match at Cowdray Park in West Sussex, and at the Braemar Gathering, the highlight of the Highland Games season.

After the Gathering, Diana caught the afternoon flight back to London with two men who would figure largely in her life – Nicholas Soames, an Equerry to Charles (and a Minister in Britain's

Above: Diana's romance with Prince Charles catapulted her into the headlines.

Above: Just a few weeks before the announcement of her engagement in 1981, Diana is seen with her colleagues at the Young England kindergarten in Pimlico. Below: Outside her Kensington flat.

Above: Diana was proud to be a bridesmaid at the wedding of her sister Lady Jane to Robert Fellowes at the Guard's Chapel in London in April 1978.

Conservative Government) and Colonel Andrew Parker Bowles, the husband of Camilla – who later loomed large in Diana's life.

For a short while, Diana's life in London continued as normal. Every morning she and her flatmates – Ann Bolton, Carolyn Pride and Virginia Pitman – took turns going for the morning newspapers and milk for breakfast. But not for long. The Press were on to Charles' girl – this 'Lady Di', as they dubbed her – and tracked her down to Coleherne Court, where battalions of reporters and cameramen pitched camp around the clock. From then on, the lenses hardly ever left her.

Among the best-known pictures of the Princess taken at the time was of her at the kindergarten where she worked, with one child balanced on her hip and the sunlight shining through her dress. 'Diaphanous Di' looked stunning, shy, beguiling, and a popular myth is that photographers 'set her up' for this picture.

Not true, according to those who were there. She was simply walking by some bushes, and the photographers took their pictures. Only later, when the film was developed, did they realise her legs could be seen so well.

Above: Diana and Camilla Parker Bowles – companionship was to turn to rivalry.

Above: The famous picture of 'Diaphanous Di' was taken at the Young England kindergarten in 1980. Reportedly its publication made Diana cry.

Diana falls in love with the man who will be King

As the weeks went on, Diana continued to enchant and enthral all who met her, and huge pressure was being put on Prince Charles to do something about the delightful girl who many believed to be the perfect mate for him.

Of her first meeting with Charles, Diana remembered: 'He was just somebody who was always around. I don't remember a great deal about it. But I do know that it was when I was still wearing nappies. It's funny, but the best things happened to me when I was still in nappies!'

But her first proper meeting with the Prince came much later, when she was a gawky 16-year-old and he was courting her sister Sarah. 'I remember being podgy, no make-up, an unsmart lady', she said. 'But I made a lot of noise and he seemed to like that.'

Another meeting came when she was invited to stay with friends at Petworth, in West Sussex, in July, 1980. She sat next to Charles on a hay bale and commiserated with him over the death of Earl Mountbatten. 'You looked so sad when you walked up the aisle at the funeral,' she told him. 'It was the most tragic thing I've ever seen. My heart bled for you when I watched it. I thought "It's wrong. You are lonely. You should be with somebody to look after you".'

A series of dates followed, and by December that year there were rumours that an engagement announcement was imminent. James Whitaker talked to Diana for a long time about the situation: 'She would not commit herself to anything', he recalls, 'But she assured me that marrying into the Royal Family would not be a problem for her. She made it clear that as she was literally brought up next door to Sandringham House, she was used to the Royal Family.'

Even so, the new pressure on her was enormous. Her phone never stopped ringing and she was followed everywhere by photographers. In public she bore the attention bravely. She told the pressmen: 'I like to think I get on very well with most of you. The only thing that really annoys me is when my children (at the kindergarten) get frightened by things like flashguns.'

Behind the scenes, though, the constant pressure was taking its toll, even in those early days: 'I cried like a baby to the four walls,' she confessed. 'I just couldn't cope with it.'

On February 6, 1981 Charles formally proposed to Diana at Windsor Castle, and that night she plonked herself down on her bed and asked her flatmates: 'Guess what?'

'He asked you?', they yelled. 'He did', she laughed, 'and I said "Yes, please!" I never had any doubts about it.' Soon afterwards she moved forever from Coleherne Court, begging her flatmates to keep in touch. 'I'll need you more than ever now', she said, as she headed off to Clarence House, official London home of the Queen Mother, where

> *"I remember being podgy…an unsmart lady. But I made a lot of noise and he seemed to like that."*

she was to stay until the marriage.

The engagement was announced three weeks later and the happy couple appeared together on TV, with Diana proudly showing off her engagement ring and her enchanting shyness. 'Are you in love?' the interviewer asked. 'Of course', Diana replied. 'Whatever love is', added the Prince wryly.

Later, it was said that Diana had reservations about the match, even up to the eleventh hour – and that she had to be persuaded to go ahead with it by her sisters, with their half-joking jests that the souvenir tea-towels were already on sale.

But if there were doubts about the wisdom of a match between a shy nursery school assistant and a settled bachelor who had been raised to become king, no-one voiced them at the time.

Above: Preparations for the wedding occupied the spring months of 1981. Here Diana and Prince Charles are seen on the steps of St Paul's Cathedral in London.

Above: The happy couple posed for photographers on the garden steps at Buckingham Palace after the official announcement of their engagement was made on February 24, 1981. Charles had proposed to Diana at Windsor Castle less than three weeks earlier.

Far left: The official engagement picture was taken by Lord Snowdon. Diana's ring featured a large sapphire surrounded by glittering diamonds.

This page (clockwise from above): Charles and Diana take a break at Balmoral before the wedding; seen together in informal mood returning to the Prince's car; at their first public engagement together – a gala charity concert in aid of the Royal Opera House held at Goldsmith's Hall in London; and Diana embracing the Duke of Kent at the Wimbledon Lawn Tennis Championships in 1981, shortly before her wedding day.

Above: On the second day of Royal Ascot, June 17, 1981, Diana appeared with the Queen and the Queen Mother wearing a delicate peach skirt and top. By now, all eyes were on her.

"Are you in love?"
"Of course." Diana replied.
"Whatever love is," added
the Prince wryly.

Right: Diana and Princess Anne at a polo match at Windsor Great Park. As a result of an accident in childhood, Diana did not much enjoy the sport of riding.
Below: As Diana began to find her feet in the public eye, her sense of poise and self-assurance blossomed.

The Fairytale that Faded so Soon

"*I always had my doubts about how he really felt. There was never anything concrete for me to grab a hold of, but I did have these feelings about things, that things weren't quite right…One minute I was a nobody. The next minute I was Princess of Wales…it was just too much for one person to handle.*"

Joy for the world – and the 'luckiest girl'

Fairytale. It's an easy, glitzy word, not least for headline writers. But this time, strangely, it seemed to fit the scenario perfectly: the bachelor prince, after a string of well-publicised romances, had at last found his true love, and she was beautiful and beguiling and becomingly shy and they'd live happily ever after.

Except, of course, as we now know, that even as they talked of love on television, the Prince was having a relationship with Camilla Parker Bowles, an old girlfriend who had married someone else.

Despite that the wedding ('of the century', as some inevitably described it) at St Paul's Cathedral on July 29, 1981, was a model of the pomp and pageantry at which the British excel. They nervously muddled each other's names. Even the Archbishop of Canterbury said it was 'the stuff of fairy tales'. And that long, lingering kiss on the Buckingham Palace balcony made front pages in news-

> *"I thought I was the luckiest girl in the world when I looked at Charles through my veil. I had tremendous hope in my heart."*

papers and magazines around the globe.

Diana remembered that before the wedding there had been her first official engagement – a London charity gala. 'It was a horrendous occasion', she said. 'I hadn't a clue what I was meant to be doing. I know people think all sorts of people gave me lessons…but they didn't. Nobody helped me at all.'

One person she met that night sympathised: Princess Grace of Monaco laughed and told Diana: 'Don't worry – it will get a lot worse'. They posed with Charles for pictures – Grace looking every inch Her Serene Highness, and Diana appearing shy and nervous in the presence of the former Hollywood film star who'd swapped her role as Grace Kelly to become a fairytale princess when she married Prince Rainier of Monaco.

Their lives, Diana could not help but reflect, were running on remarkably similar courses – and she shared the world's shock and sadness when, in the September of the following year, Princess Grace was killed in a horrifying car crash, leaving her husband

Above: A proud father escorts his daughter up the aisle at St Paul's Cathedral.

Above: Amid all the excitement of her wedding day, Princess Diana finds a moment to talk to her bridesmaids on their return to Buckingham Palace after the church ceremony.

Above: The fairytale wedding: Diana travelled from Clarence House to St Paul's in the Glass Coach, a suitably romantic conveyance for such a leading lady.

and young family to grieve for an attractive and much-loved woman who had done so much, and on an international scale, to help others less fortunate than herself.

As her wedding day approached, Diana became increasingly nervous: 'In 12 days' time I shall no longer be me', she told her dance teacher. And on the day itself she woke early for what she later described as 'the most emotionally confusing day of my life'.

She said: 'I thought I was the luckiest girl in the world when I looked at Charles through my veil. I had tremendous hope in my heart. At the age of 19 you always think you're prepared for everything, and you think you know what's coming.

'No-one sat me down with a piece of paper and said "This is what's expected of you."

Left: Diana and her Prince leaving the Cathedral. The wedding dress, designed by the Emanuels, was the talk of the moment.

But although I was daunted by the prospect at the time, I felt I had the support of my husband-to-be.'

Diana believed she had found her fairy-tale prince – and when she walked down the aisle, the world believed it, too. Swathed in oceans of ivory silk taffetta and with diamonds sparkling in her hair, she looked the perfect partner for Charles, resplendent in his Royal Navy uniform.

And their lavish wedding – in a year which had seen unprecedented violence in the inner cities of Britain – brought joy throughout the realm and to millions more around the world.

The newlyweds spent the first three days of their honeymoon at Broadlands, the peaceful Hampshire home of the Mountbatten family. But Diana's hopes of an idyllic romantic few days away from the media spotlight had already been dashed when her husband packed his fishing rods and half a dozen books.

This page: The newly married couple's return journey to Buckingham Palace through the streets of London was met with an outpouring of public acclaim and affection. The humanity and tenderness of the new Princess shone through all the pomp and circumstance and the pageantry.

Right: A radiant Princess Diana – all nervousness has been dispelled and her expression is one of sheer happiness.

After Broadlands they set off for a cruise of the Mediterranean aboard the royal yacht *Britannia*, which should have reinforced the commitment of a couple who had come to marriage in need of love and warmth and affection. But from the start it was clear that there would be massive problems to overcome.

Diana was determined to make it work: 'I think like any marriage, especially when you've had divorced parents like mine, you want to try even harder to make it work', she said. 'And you don't want to fall back into a pattern that you've seen happen in your own family.

'I desperately wanted it to work. I desperately loved my husband and I wanted to share everything together, and I thought that we were a very good team.'

But even on the honeymoon the cracks were starting to appear in the marriage as the presence of Camilla Parker Bowles in Charles' life became all too clear to Diana. She broke down and wept one day when two photographs of Camilla fell out of her new husband's diary.

Diana begged him to tell her the truth about his relationship with Camilla and how he felt about his new wife. But her pleas were ignored, and Charles gave no explanation, leaving her desperately unhappy, unsure and confused.

Even worse was the painful evening during the honeymoon when the couple entertained Egyptian President Anwar Sadat and his wife Jihan – and Charles arrived for dinner wearing a new pair of cufflinks in the shape of two interwoven Cs.

He said the gift from Camilla was merely a token of her friendship and nothing for his new bride to worry about. But Diana told friends later: 'I could not see why Charles needed these constant reminders of Camilla'.

After the honeymoon cruise, the couple returned to join the rest of the royal family for their traditional annual holiday on the Balmoral estate from August until October – and Diana hoped against hope that the media attention in her would now wane, if only a little.

Above and below: The famous kiss on the balcony of Buckingham Palace – a moment of spontaneity amid all the protocol and pageantry.

Above: Lord Lichfield's photograph of the Prince and Princess surrounded by their young bridesmaids and pages, and with best man Prince Andrew and Prince Edward, has a slightly informal feel that captures the joy of a young couple in love.

Right: The royal couple about to board an aircraft on the way to Gibraltar where they joined the royal yacht Britannia *for their honeymoon cruise in the Mediterranean.*

'When we were married they said that it would go quiet', she said. 'It didn't. And then it started to focus very much on me, and seemed to be on the front page of a newspaper every single day, which is an isolating experience.

'It took a long time to understand why people were so interested in me, but I assumed it was because my husband had done a lot of wonderful work leading up to our marriage. But then during the years you see yourself as a good product that sits on a shelf and sells well, and people make a lot of money out of you.'

She added: 'I was very daunted, because as far as I was concerned I was a fat, chubby, 20-year-old, and I couldn't understand the level of interest.'

> *"One minute I was a nobody. The next minute I was Princess of Wales, mother, media toy, member of this family."*

While at Balmoral the rows over Camilla continued. In public, they smiled for the cameras and Diana said she 'highly recommended married life'. But inside she was struggling with the knowledge that her husband was in love with someone else.

How did she cope? Much later she would say: 'I've got what my mother has got. However bloody you are feeling, you can put on the most amazing show of happiness. My mother is an expert at that and I've picked it up. It kept the wolves from the door'.

And of Charles, she said: 'I always had my doubts about how he really felt. There was never anything concrete for me to grab a hold of, but I did have these feelings about things, that things weren't quite right.'

Camilla was not the only problem in the marriage, though. Not least of the others was the 12-year age gap. She was a 20-year-old, young for her years, and he a 32-year-old who already seemed middle-aged. They had different characters, different desires, different enthusiasms. His older, wiser, friends intimidated and bored her. Her younger, brighter, set irritated him.

She did not much care for his polo or his country pursuits, which were the centre of his family's life. He was far from at home in discos or on the dance floor. And the differences soon put a great strain on the royal marriage.

Above and below: The honeymoon ends – a relaxed couple at Balmoral, August 1981.

Above: Aboard Britannia. *Charles and Diana spent 12 days cruising in the Mediterranean. Outwardly all seemed amicable, but already Charles' friendship with Camilla Parker Bowles was casting a shadow.*

Diana, abruptly removed from those happy, giggling, girlish days at the Coleherne Court flat to the strict conformity of court life, told her old friends she felt bewildered and lost. The building was remote, the courtiers unapproachable, the way of life stuffy and staid beyond belief. Even the intensive royal round of official home and foreign visits brought their own particular problem.

The huge crowds, Charles very soon came to realise, were turning out to see his glamorous new wife rather than him. Her presence electrified crowds and left him feeling left out of it: 'I might just as well stay in the car', he grumbled. But the crowds were creating problems for Diana, too.

The shy teenager quickly became a woman of violent mood swings, according to Charles' biographer, Jonathan Dimbleby. And often she would be in tears, saying she simply could not cope, as they travelled on to yet another royal appointment.

Diana became the 'Prisoner of Wales', trapped and frightened in an alien environment, and began to suffer from the slimmer's disease bulimia nervosa, characterised by bouts of binge eating and purging, which drove her to attempt to take her own life on more than one occasion.

Desperately trying to fit into the family

Soon after their honeymoon, as the couple posed for pictures on the banks of the River Dee, Di looked as thin as she had been in the weeks leading up to the wedding. But no-one was concerned. It was, after all, a demanding time for the girl.

And she was trying, desperately, to fit in. On their first official tour together, in the Principality of Wales, it never stopped raining and everyone was soaked. But Diana refused to wear an overcoat or mac, insisting that the public wanted to see her.

She was an instant smash hit by just being herself – no-one in the royal family had taught her anything, she said – and the crowd loved her for it. She was great at small talk and with the young kids and older people, and she never once complained about the appalling weather except in a jokey fashion. Diana-mania had begun.

But behind the scenes, a different picture of a deeply troubled Princess was emerging. Author Andrew Morton later claimed she slashed at her wrists with a razor blade, a penknife and a lemon slicer and once threw herself against a glass cabinet.

In January 1981, six months into the marriage and pregnant with William, she threw herself down the stairs at Sandringham. The Queen Mother was the first to arrive at the scene and was very shaken at what had happened. But Diana was lucky: she suffered severe bruising to her stomach, but she – and the baby she was carrying – were otherwise unharmed.

It was, she explained later, a cry for help: 'When no-one listens to you, or you feel no-one's listening to you, all sorts of things start to happen. For instance, you have so much pain inside yourself that you try and hurt yourself on the outside because you want help, but it's the wrong help you're asking for.

'People see it as crying wolf or attention-seeking, and they think because you're in the media all the time you've got enough attention…but I was actually crying out because I wanted to get better in order to go forward and continue my duty and my role as wife, mother, Princess of Wales. So yes,

Above: Diana's first child, William, was born on June 21, 1982 at St Mary's Hospital, Paddington.

I did inflict harm upon myself. I didn't like myself, I was ashamed because I couldn't cope with the pressures.'

During the next few weeks, before William was born in June, Diana suffered badly. She did not have a happy pregnancy, suffering from morning sickness, but continued with her public engagements and enchanted everyone she met.

It was a very frail-looking Diana who appeared on the steps of the hospital with William in her arms. And Charles appeared distant. Asked about married life, he said: 'It's all right, but it interferes with my hunting'.

Diana said of the birth: 'I felt the whole country was in labour with me. I felt enormous relief. But I had actually known William was going to be a boy, because the scan had

shown it. So it caused no surprise.'

She added: 'When William arrived it was a great relief because it was all peaceful again, and I was well for a time'. But motherhood brought new pressures: 'One minute I was a nobody. The next minute I was Princess of Wales, mother, media toy, member of this family and...it was just too much for one person to handle.

Left and above: Four generations of a Royal Family on the occasion of William's christening, and the Queen Mother's birthday, on August 4, 1982.

Far left: Visiting Ayer's Rock on March 21, 1983 during the Royal Tour of Australia.
Left: Whenever she went walkabout, Diana was very much the star attraction, evidently somewhat to Prince Charles' chagrin.
Below: At the opening of the St John Ambulance Regional Centre in Alice Springs.

'Then I was unwell with post-natal depression, which no-one ever discusses. You have to read about it afterwards, and that in itself was a bit of a difficult time. You'd wake up in the morning and you didn't want to get out of bed. You felt misunderstood and just very, very low in yourself.

'I never had a depression in my life. But then when I analysed it I could see that the changes I'd made in the last year had all caught up with me, and my body had said "We want a rest".

'I received a great deal of treatment, but I knew in myself that actually what I needed was space and time to adapt to all the different roles that had come my way. I knew I could do it, but I needed people to be patient and give me the space to do it.

'It was a very short space of time. In the space of a year my whole life had changed, been turned upside down, and it had its wonderful moments. And I could see where the rough edges needed to be smoothed.'

Diana understood how her depression might have been daunting for the royal family: 'Maybe I was the first person ever to be in the family who ever had a depression or was ever openly tearful. And obviously that was daunting, because if you've never seen it before, how do you support it?'

Nothing, though, must interfere with royal duties, and in early 1983 Diana's duty was

Above: Just over two years after the birth of William, on September 15, 1984 Prince Harry was born. Here Charles and Diana leave St Mary's Hospital with him.

Above: Diana and Charles hold the month-old baby William. It is revealing to compare Diana's appearance in this photograph with the sophisticated woman carrying Harry (above left).

to tour Australia and New Zealand with her husband. The Royal Family wanted her to go without William. But she would not think of it. If she went, her new child had to go, too.

Buckingham Palace did not like the idea, but it worked. After landing in Australia, Diana installed William with nanny Barbara Barnes at a house in New South Wales and travelled there with Charles whenever they had a spare moment. In between, she carried out all her engagements and was a triumph wherever she went.

For Charles, though, it emphasised his second-billing status in public affection whenever he appeared with his wife. Crowds lining both sides of the street would groan when Charles was on their side. 'You've got me', he'd tell them, 'You'd better ask for your money back.' But he felt surplus to requirements and he didn't like it.

Nor did the Princess's progress from popular idol to semi-saint, achieved through her remarkable personal warmth as comforter of the sick, the dying and the needy, come easy for her husband. But she won worldwide acclaim for her espousal of the cause of AIDS victims, doing much to dispel the common belief that social contacts, such as shaking hands, could spread the disease.

And the British Government, realising that she was a major asset to the nation, could

Above: From Australia, the royal tour moved on to New Zealand. On April 23, William and his parents faced the cameras on the lawn of Government House in Auckland.

Above: The White House meets Saturday Night Fever – during the royal visit to America in 1985 Diana danced with John Travolta at a Washington gala. 'I'll give her ten out of ten', he enthused.
Right: Dancing the night away, Charles and Diana take to the floor.
Far Right: As a child Diana dreamed of becoming a ballerina. Here she appears on stage with Wayne Sleep for charity in 1985.

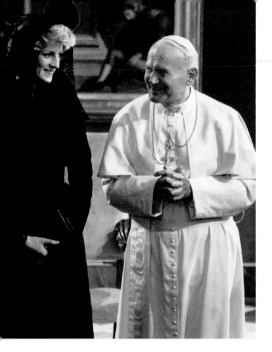

Above: Diana exhibits her wicked sense of fun, and Charles seems to be enjoying the joke.
Below: At the Live Aid concert in 1985. Diana greatly enjoyed rock music and live concerts.

Top: Diana and Pope Paul II, 1985.
Above: A public display of affection at a
Windsor polo match in 1983.

not wait to get her into a country to help boost goodwill and exports. The tours came in quick succession: to Spain, to France, a magnificent two-week visit to Italy, to Portugal, to America and later to Brazil, Japan and India.

But within the Royal Family, the Princess seems to have been regarded as an uncontrollable 'wild card' and to have been isolated accordingly. No single event can be said to have caused the breakdown of the marriage. The Prince told TV viewers that he was faithful to Diana until the relationship had 'irretrievably broken down' in the second half of the 80s.

The Princess's estimate of when the marriage died is earlier. She says it was effectively over after the birth of her second son, Prince Harry, in September 1984. Charles had hoped for a girl, and a dismissive remark – 'Oh it's a boy and he's even got rusty hair' – marked the beginning of the end. 'From that moment, something inside me died', the Princess told friends.

Rage and rows were reported as commonplace. The Prince stuck rigidly to his annual schedule of polo, hunting, shooting and fishing, regardless of school holidays or family weekends. The Princess sank into the trough of bulimia.

Charles, taught from birth to keep his feelings under a tight rein and to himself, hid his unhappiness behind the mask of his royal duty. But his wife – more emotional, more theatrical, too highly strung and less well trained – was unable to camouflage her distress.

She grew to loathe the dinner parties Charles gave at Kensington Palace. She had little in common with many of the guests, was no gourmet and didn't particularly like wine – except in bursts, when she would binge on certain drinks.

Eventually she began going to bed before the party broke up, and after a year or two of trying her best – which wasn't good enough

– she started missing the dinner parties altogether. She acquired a young set of friends, more her own age, to spend time with. People like James Gilbey, a motor racing man with whom she had the famous 'Squidgy' telephone conversation, and Guards officers like Major David Waterhouse. She led a lonely existence. Occasionally she would go to the cinema at High Street Kensington, but often she would curl up at home with a book and get to bed early.

It seemed that the whole world was in love with Diana except her husband, and as a substitute for this lonely existence, she took on more and more engagements on behalf of her many charities – and worked out even harder in various gyms.

People who criticised her for going out to gyms and running the gauntlet of the dreaded paparazzi each morning didn't understand her need to get out from Kensington Palace. She felt cooped up there, incredibly frustrated.

'She has this great urge to go out and meet real people', an aide explained. 'Of course she could have a private gym at the palace, but she finds the place a little bit like prison.'

At the same time, Diana's relationship with her family was proving very difficult. Originally she got on very well with her mother, but in recent years that relationship had deteriorated. And in the last few months she was quite hostile about Frances Shand Kydd.

She was furious when Mrs Shand Kydd

> "She has this great urge to go out and meet real people. Of course she could have a private gym at the palace, but she finds the place a bit like a prison."

gave an interview in which she expressed the opinion that Diana was upset about the HRH tag being removed during her divorce settlement. At the same time, Diana's relationships with her brother Charles and sisters Sarah and Jane were up and down.

Volatile redhead Lady Sarah was once lady-in-waiting for Diana, but they didn't always get on that well. There was ever-present sibling rivalry – and always a bit of a problem that Sarah had been the girlfriend of Charles before Diana.

With brother Charles, Diana was unhappy when she was refused permission to create a home at the family seat, Althorp – and equally distraught at the breakdown of Charles' marriage to Victoria, and their subsequent departure for South Africa.

Top and above: By the mid-80s the strains in the marriage were taking their toll. However, in public photocalls, particularly with the children, appearances were maintained.

Above: Prince William's first day at his nursery school – an anxious occasion for pupil and mother alike.

Left and above: Diana relaxes with William and Harry during a summer holiday in Majorca in 1987. As a member of the Royal Family with a daunting schedule of appearances to undergo month after month, Diana cherished the time that she could spend in private with her sons, free from the pressures of public engagements, if not from the attentions of press photographers.

Seeking solace in the company of others

With Jane there was a problem, too. She is the easiest-going of all the Spencer children, but she is married to Sir Robert Fellowes, who is totally supportive of the Queen and took the royal side when it came to the divorce.

During the mid 80s, when the Prince and Princess were taking William and Harry on bucket-and-spade holidays to Majorca as guests of King Juan Carlos and the Queen of Spain, there was little physical or mental rapport between the two of them. And it was the events witnessed during a sunshine holiday in the summer of 1986 which first publicly exposed the growing cracks in the marriage.

> *"Are Charles and Di still in tune?" Buckingham Palace insisted everything was fine. But friends have said that after this trip to Majorca, the couple never slept together again.*

Out for a day's cruise off Palma, Majorca, they did not exchange a single word with one another for the seven hours they spent on King Juan Carlos' motor yacht, the *Fortuna*. When Charles came up on deck Diana went below, and vice versa. Diana swam alone, Charles wind-surfed all by himself.

He came home three days early from Majorca, leaving behind his wife and sons, then aged four and two, and it was said that

he was going fishing. But many later believed the real reason was that he wanted to join Camilla Parker Bowles in Scotland.

Newspapers asked, 'Are Charles and Di still in tune?' Buckingham Palace insisted everything was fine. But friends have said that after this trip to Majorca, the couple never slept together again.

Her husband's early departure set a pattern that was to become familiar over the next six years. They spoke little and appeared to go out of their way to avoid each other's company. At a polo match, Charles kissed his wife after losing a game. She scornfully wiped her lips with the back of her hand. Then, said witnesses, there was an extraordinary scene in the car park, where Diana appeared to kick out at her husband and he shoved her back against her car.

Elsewhere, all was going well enough. Diana was involved in numerous charities as Patron or President, and was a triumph, helping to raise millions of pounds for the organisations she was spearheading. And she was tireless in helping the disadvantaged and the poor.

When she attended an engagement she would always overrun her allotted time. Each child got a pat on the head, each mother or father kind words. She was faultless.

But Diana also began to feed on the adulation and adoration that the public gave her, and in some ways she no longer needed Prince Charles. By the end of the 80s he was no longer there for her.

Not for one moment, many believe, did Charles contemplate divorce, but emotionally he was involved with only one woman – Camilla Parker Bowles. And by now Diana had taken her own lover, James Hewitt.

The good-looking ex-cavalry officer had helped teach William and Harry to ride – and at the same time won the Princess' broken heart. In her infamous *Panorama* interview,

Above: Diana clowns with the Duchess of York on the ski slopes.
Right: Sarah Ferguson was another royal bride who challenged Palace orthodoxy.

Diana talked of how much she had 'adored' Hewitt in a relationship said to have lasted from 1986 until 1991. She also sought friendship with used-car dealer James Gilbey.

The Prince continued to see Camilla – by ironic coincidence the great-granddaughter of Alice Keppel, mistress of Charles' great-great grandfather, Edward VII. And no-one seemed surprised when in 1988 author Anthony Holden published a biography portraying the royal relationship as a marriage of convenience.

Throughout 1988, the Princess was treated by eminent London psychiatrist Dr Maurice Lipsedge, sometimes for days at a time. He broke her dependency on the gorging and

This page (clockwise from top): The family on holiday in the Scilly Isles; Prince Harry's first day at Wetherby School; Diana competing in the mother's race at Wetherby School in 1990.

Above: Diana and her sons came to love winter sports in the Alps. Here they are seen on a chair lift at Lech in Austria in 1992.

rejection of food, which is the foundation of bulimia.

Friends say he made her see that the illness was a result of inner depression and insecurity and that, once she conquered that, the physical illness could be dealt with. And it was.

But the marriage had become a tyranny of togetherness and seemed beyond treatment. Had they been an ordinary couple, they would undoubtedly have divorced years earlier.

They were christened 'The Glums'. The Princess looked positively gloomy at her husband's side, yet relaxed and friendly on her own. Charles, in turn, appeared cold and uninterested in his wife.

> *By 1991 the marriage was teetering on the edge, with a former royal policeman revealing: "They never smile, laugh or do anything together. They seem to want as little contact as possible."*

By 1991 the marriage was teetering on the edge, with former royal policeman Andrew Jacques revealing: 'They never smile, laugh or do anything together. They seem to want as little contact as possible.'

In February 1992 they made a trip to India, where the Prince and Princess were not only in separate bedrooms but on separate floors of their palace. And the signs of open hostility between them were becoming more and more apparent.

On one truly grim day the couple split, with Charles staying behind in Delhi to address businessmen while Diana went off to Agra to visit Shah Jahan's magnificent Taj Mahal, the world's most romantic monument to love.

Diana made a huge point while at this mausoleum. She posed all alone in front of the edifice and looked downcast and forlorn. And Charles was left explaining that he'd not made a wise decision staying behind in the capital.

Too true. And a few days later, on the eve of St Valentine's Day, Diana made her biggest point ever when she turned her head away at the end of a polo match in Jaipur when Charles went to kiss her. He ended up brushing her ear, totally humiliated.

Above and top: As the marriage crumbled, Diana devoted more and more of her efforts to charity work. Her rapport with children was obvious in her visit to a deprived area in Brazil in 1991.

Top: Meeting the world famous tenor Luciano Pavarotti after his open-air concert in Hyde Park.
Above: Two ladies of mercy meet in Rome in February 1992. Mother Teresa died just five days
after Diana, on September 5, 1997.

In March 1992 Diana received devastating news – of the death of her much-loved father – while she was skiing in Lech, Austria, and Charles offered to fly back to Britain with her. She told him: 'It's a bit late to start acting the caring husband'.

But the Queen demanded that Diana allow Charles to accompany her, and she relented. The couple travelled together to Kensington Palace – and Charles immediately took off for Highgrove, leaving Diana to mourn alone.

A friend said 'Charles only flew home with her for the sake of his public image. She felt that at a time when she was grieving the death of her father, she should be given the opportunity of behaving as she wanted, rather than go through this masquerade.'

The cracks in the marriage had split wide open, and joint visits were not as many as before, but there was one ghastly tour still to come – to Korea in November, when the frostiness between them was awful to behold. After a couple of days it was as if they were on separate tours of the same country.

> *"We struggled along, we did our engagements together. And in our private life it was obviously turbulent."*

Separation, if not divorce, was on the cards, and it was almost incidental that the Duke of York's marriage was heading for disaster, too. With the divorce from Mark Phillips by Princess Anne, the three married Windsor children were in a terrible mess.

All the Windsor family values, as encouraged so much by Queen Victoria, were in a shambles. But the only one that really mattered was the marriage of the Waleses. And that was about to be hit by the publication of Andrew Morton's bombshell book *Diana: Her True Story*.

Left: While Diana struggled to maintain a composed public face, inside her emotions were in turmoil. Here she is seen during the ceremony of Trooping the Colour in 1992.
Below: The pensive look is suggestive of inner troubles. One of the penalties of fame is that private anguish cannot be kept from the public eye.

Above: Cruising in the sun on King Juan Carlos' yacht Fortuna *off Palma, Majorca in 1986, but the atmosphere between Charles and Diana was frosty.*

Written with her tacit consent, it portrayed a lonely, neurotic princess, driven to tears, bulimia and tantrums by her unhappy marriage. It exposed the prince as a distant father, uncaring husband and adulterer.

The book disclosed that, even as the fairy-tale couple had honeymooned on the royal yacht *Britannia*, the prince was in regular touch with his long-time companion and mistress, Mrs Parker Bowles.

Doubts about the origin of the Morton revelations were quashed when, three days after the first extract of the book was published, the princess paid a visit to her friend Carolyn Bartholomew, who had furnished much telling material for the book.

Diana thought the book might help: 'I was at the end of my tether', she said. 'I was des-

Above: A mother's love – Diana's joy on being reunited with Wills and Harry during a tour of Canada in 1991 is plain to see.

perate. I think I was so fed up with being seen as someone who was a basket case, because I am a very strong person and I know that causes complications in the system I live in.'

After the book, though, 'maybe people have a better understanding. Maybe there's a lot of women out there who suffer on the same level, but in a different environment, who are unable to stand up for themselves because their self-esteem is cut in two.'

The Morton book, she agreed, had been devastating: 'I think the royal family were shocked and horrified and very disappointed. What had been hidden, or rather what we thought had been hidden, then came out in the open and was spoken about on a daily basis, and the pressure was for us to sort ourselves out in some way.

'Were we going to stay together, or were we going to separate? And the word separation and divorce kept coming up in the media on a daily basis. We struggled along. We did our engagements together. And in our private life it was obviously turbulent.'

The princess continued to maintain her extraordinary hold on public sympathy and affection despite the publication of tapes of intimate telephone conversations, known as the 'Squidgy Affair', apparently between her and James Gilbey, whose voice could be heard professing love.

And that disastrous tour of Korea by the ill-at-ease Prince and Princess in November 1992 sealed the fate of the marriage. It was plain to all that the marriage of the royal Glums was all but over.

In fact talks about their future were going on behind the scenes. Press speculation of a split was never-ending. And Diana was telling a woman friend in a private conversation (which later was said to have been bugged by MI5): 'I've been acting the biggest role of

Above: In sombre mood after Charles' skiing companions had been killed in an accident in Klosters in 1988.
Right: Diana in tears shortly after the publication of Andrew Morton's book.

my career for 10 years. I should be in movies. I'm going. So are the boys. It's an impossible situation.'

But she denied rumours that she was demanding her own palace: 'All I want is Charles to leave Kensington Palace', she said. 'We could see what the public were requiring. They wanted clarity in a situation that was obviously becoming intolerable.

'So we got the lawyers together, we discussed separation. Obviously there were a lot of people to discuss it with – the Prime Minister, Her Majesty – and then it moved itself, so to speak.'

By December they had agreed to a legal separation and it was announced by Buckingham Palace and in the House of Commons by Prime Minister John Major, who said there were no plans for a divorce.

For Diana it brought 'deep, deep, profound sadness. Because we had struggled to

Above and right: The official tour of Korea in November 1992 marked the low-water mark of the marriage. The estrangement of the couple was all too clear to see; on account of their miserable demeanour, the Wales were nicknamed the Glums by the press travelling with them on this tour.

Above: A poignant scene – the last family Christmas card, dating from 1991. The photograph was taken by Lord Snowdon.

keep it going, but obviously we'd both run out of steam. And in a way I suppose it could have been a relief for us both that we'd finally made our minds up.

'But my husband asked for the separation and I supported it. I came from a divorced background and I didn't want to go into that one again.'

Of the children, she said: 'I asked my husband if we could put the announcement out before they came back from school for Christmas holidays, because they were protected in the school they were at. I went down a week beforehand and explained what was happening.

'And they took it as children do – asking lots of questions – and I hoped I was able to reassure them. But who knows?

'I think the announcement had a huge effect on me and Charles, and the children were very much out of it, in the sense that they were tucked away at school.

'I take some responsibility that our marriage went the way it did. I'll take half of it, but I won't take any more than that, because it takes two to get in this situation. We both made mistakes.'

News of the royal split was announced as Diana was working. 'I was on an engagement up North', she remembered. 'I heard it on the radio, and it was just very, very sad. Really sad. The fairytale had come to an end.'

Above and right: On the tour of India in February 1992 signs of open hostility between the couple became obvious to see. Princess Diana turned her head away when Charles made to kiss her. And in a move that must have been calculated to engage public sympathy, Diana posed alone and forlorn in front of the Taj Mahal, the most spectacular monument to marital love and fidelity in the world.

"I've taken the children to all sorts of areas where I'm not sure anyone of that age in

Where do I go from Here?

this family has been before…And they have a knowledge – they may never use it, but the seed is there – and I hope it will grow, because knowledge is power. I want them to have an understanding of people's emotions, people's insecurities, people's distress and people's hopes and dreams."

Now it's OK to be different

Diana was alone, again, and trying to come to terms with her new and unique role, as the separated wife of the Prince of Wales and mother to his sons, one the future King.

She told friends: 'Inside the system I was treated very differently, as though I was an oddball. I felt I wasn't good enough. Now, thank God, it's OK to be different.'

But the separation brought tensions and suspicion on both sides. Diana had her home swept for listening devices and spent a lot of time fretting about Charles' plans. She felt people had changed in their attitude towards

– the first when transcripts of telephone calls between her and James Gilbey were mysteriously leaked to the Press.

In the infamous 'Squidgytapes', Diana is heard to say: 'I don't want to get pregnant'. He replies: 'Darling, that's not going to happen'. But Diana says: 'I watched *Eastenders* today. One of the main characters had a baby. They thought it was by her husband. It was by another man.'

Asked later, in the famous BBC *Panorama* programme, if the transcript was accurate, Diana replied: 'Yes. He is a very affectionate person. But the implications of that conversation were that we'd had an adulterous relationship, which was not true.'

How, then, had the conversation come to

Above: In the now famous Panorama *interview in November 1995 Diana told her side of the story, baring her soul to the nation in the process.*

> "*Inside the system I was treated very differently, as though I was an oddball. I felt I wasn't good enough.*"

her: 'I was now the separated wife of the Prince of Wales. I was a problem, a liability. How are we going to deal with her? This hasn't happened before.

'It showed itself by visits abroad being blocked. By things that had come naturally my way being stopped, letters that got lost, and various things. Everything changed after we separated, and life became very difficult for me. My husband's side were very busy stopping me.'

And the Press, and the public, were very busy wondering who would be the new man in her life. Before long Diana was being assailed by juicy stories about her private life

Above and left: Diana announced her withdrawal from public engagements and many charity commitments during a speech at London's Hilton Hotel in 1993.

Above: Photographers clamour for pictures at the Hilton engagement in December 1993.

Diana and the princes, accompanied by a detective, 'shooting the rapids' at Thorpe Park in 1992.

be published? Diana had no idea. 'But it was done to harm me in a serious manner, and that was the first time I'd experienced what it was like to be outside the net, so to speak, and not be in the family.

'It was to make the public change their attitude towards me. It was, you know, if we are going to divorce, my husband would hold more cards than I would. It was very much a poker game, a chess game.'

Diana believed there was a campaign to discredit her. 'She won't go quietly, that's the

problem.' But she promised: 'I'll fight to the end, because I believe I have a role to fulfil, and I've got two children to bring up.'

Later in 1993 came another sensational tape – the intimate late-night telephone call between Prince Charles and Camilla Parker Bowles, in which they declared their undying love for each other. But what infuriated Diana about it was the mention of so many people who'd conspired with the lovers to deceive her by providing 'safe houses' for their meetings.

Meanwhile, nothing else seemed to be going right for her. She began to dread the endless round of tree-planting and hand-shaking. 'I'm the biggest prostitute in the world', she told a friend. 'I'm handed round like a tube of Smarties.'

Relations with some of her staff and bodyguards became strained, too, and when her valued chauffeur Simon Solari suddenly resigned to join Charles' staff, Diana burst into tears: 'It hit me when I was least expecting it', she said, and that evening she asked Solari to park by the Serpentine in Hyde Park so she could compose herself to face a charity theatre event.

It was pointless. Half an hour after the performance began, she fled the theatre, claiming she had a migraine. But next day she was back on form, joking to another charity audience about the growing rumours of her being mentally unstable.

'Ladies and gentlemen', she said, 'you are very lucky to have your patron here today. I was supposed to have my head down the loo for most of the day. I am supposed to be dragged off the minute I leave here by men in white coats. But if it's all right by you, I thought I might postpone my nervous breakdown for a more appropriate moment. It's amazing what a migraine can bring on.'

But by the end of 1993, the strain was genuine and Diana was at a low ebb. It was then she shocked her admirers by announcing her withdrawal from much of public life and her role as the figurehead of many charities.

'The pressure was intolerable', she said

The boys were a great comfort to Diana during the difficult years, and she was determined to give them as 'normal' a life as possible in return.

and space to rebuild her private life. And she pledged: 'My first priority will continue to be our children, William and Harry, who deserve as much love, care and attention as I am able to give, as well as an appreciation of the tradition into which they were born'.

To that end, Diana devised a programme to make the two princes aware of the darker side of life by taking them on visits to hostels for the homeless and people dying of AIDS. It was part of her conviction that the monarchy had to change for a modern age and that she knew the secret of how to do it.

'I've taken the children to all sorts of areas where I'm not sure anyone of that age in this

This page: More fun at Thorpe Park, where Diana's troubled private life appeared to be forgotten, if only temporarily. The young princes counted this amusement centre just outside London as their favourite.

Right: Smiles all round at the Albert Hall during Prince Harry's first public engagement as Diana encourages Harry to pluck up the courage to talk to the people to the left.

later. 'And my job, my work, was being affected. I wanted to give 110 per cent to my work and I could only give 50. I was constantly tired, exhausted because the pressure was so cruel.

'I thought the only way to do it was to stand up and make a speech and extract myself before I started disappointing and not carrying out my work. I owed it to my public to say that, you know, "Thank you. I'm disappearing for a bit. But I'll come back."'

She told her audience, at a charity lunch in London: 'When I started my public life 12 years ago, I understood that the media might be interested in what I did. I realised that their attention would inevitably focus on both our private and public lives.

'But I was not aware how overwhelming that attention would become, nor the extent to which it would affect both my public duties and my personal life in a manner that has been hard to bear.'

Although she planned to go on supporting a few charities, Diana appealed for time

Above: White-water rafting with William and Harry in Colorado, 1995. There was some media criticism of her for supposedly endangering her sons in this way.

Above: Diana and Harry accompanied William to Eton as he took his place there in 1995.

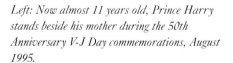

Left: Now almost 11 years old, Prince Harry stands beside his mother during the 50th Anniversary V-J Day commemorations, August 1995.

A scene that mothers the world over can identify with. Casual dress is the order of the day as Diana and Prince William drop Harry off at school.

family has been before', she said. 'And they have a knowledge – they may never use it, but the seed is there – and I hope it will grow, because knowledge is power.

'I want them to have an understanding of people's emotions, people's insecurities, people's distress and people's hopes and dreams.'

To another friend, she said: 'I want them to experience what most people already know – that they are growing up in a multi-racial society in which not everyone is rich, has four holidays a year, speaks standard English and has a Range Rover'.

She insisted that a broad knowledge of society was essential for William, the future king. 'And through learning what I do and his father does he has got an insight into what is coming his way. He's not hidden upstairs with the governess.'

Diana was full of pride when she watched William conduct himself with dignity and kindness during visits to centres for the homeless in London: 'He loves it and that really rattles people', she said.

Another time she watched as William helped entertain a group of mentally handi-

Above: Prince William looks on as Diana presents James Hewitt with a trophy at a Tidworth polo event in 1989. Right: James Gilbey, another man who featured large in her life.

Above: Princess Diana appears stressed as she gets out of her car at her Chelsea Harbour fitness club just before her Panorama *interview, November 1995.*

Left: England rugby star Will Carling's name was linked with that of the Princess after he taught her sons to play rugby in 1993.

capped children on a visit to his prep school, Ludgrove: 'I was so thrilled and proud', she smiled. 'A lot of adults couldn't handle that.

'Britain will be lucky to get William. He's all right.'

She doted on 'the boys' and felt lost when they were not with her – and the worst times were the Christmases, especially that of 1993. After greeting the crowd following the Christmas Day church service with the royal party, Diana left the boys with their father and returned to an empty Kensington Palace.

Her butler had left her Christmas dinner, which she ate alone before going for a

solitary swim at Buckingham Palace. And next day she flew, alone, to stay with her good friend Lucia Flecha de Lima. 'I cried all the way out and all the way back', she confessed. 'I felt so sorry for myself.'

Life was not much easier the following year, especially after Prince Charles admitted his adultery with Camilla Parker Bowles in his famous BBC interview with Jonthan Dimbleby.

In the two-and-a-half-hour documentary, screened in June, Charles revealed that he would never give up his mistress. 'Mrs Parker Bowles is a great friend of mine', he said. 'She's been a friend for a very long time and will continue to be for a very long time.'

Wringing his hands and constantly contorting his face, Charles said both he and Diana had desperately tried to save their

Above: A relaxed Diana at Wimbledon with her mother, Frances Shand Kydd.

marriage and 'Obviously I'd much rather it hadn't happened and I'm sure...my wife would have felt the same'.

Challenged over stories that he had been 'persistently unfaithful' in his affair with Camilla, he replied: 'These things are so personal that it is difficult to know how to talk about them'. And asked if he had tried to be 'faithful and honourable' to Diana when he took his marriage vows, he said: 'Yes, absolutely'.

But when Dimbleby asked: 'And you were?', Charles said: 'Yes, until it became irretrievably broken down, us both having tried'.

Asked if he believed the breakdown of his marriage had damaged his reputation and the monarchy, the prince said: 'Well obviously I don't recommend it to anybody'. But he dismissed as 'extraordinary' suggestions that he might abdicate, and made it clear that he intended to rule.

Then, showing sympathy for Diana's plight, he admitted that marrying into the royal family was difficult for outsiders: 'I think those who marry into my family find it increasingly difficult to do so because of the added pressure. The strains and stresses become almost intolerable.'

> *"To be honest about a relationship with someone else, in his position, that's quite something."*

Talking of William and Harry, he said he was concerned about what they read of his relationships: 'I feel strongly they should be protected as much as possible. It's important for them to develop in as private an atmosphere as possible'.

A pensive Camilla Parker Bowles pictured on the day of Charles' Panorama interview. During the two-and-a-half-hour programme he revealed that he would not give up his mistress.

Right: By attending a fund-raising dinner, Diana stole the world media's attention on the night of Prince Charles' Dimbleby interview.

Diana said the first she knew about Charles' sensational revelation about Camilla was when she saw it on television. 'And my first concern was the children, because they were able to understand what was coming out and I wanted to protect them.

'I was pretty devastated myself, but then I admired the honesty, because it takes a lot to do that. To be honest about a relationship with someone else, in his position, that's quite something.'

She explained: 'I went to the school and put it to William, particularly, that if you find someone you love in life you must hang on to it and look after it. And if you were lucky enough to find someone who loved you, then you must protect it.

'William asked me what had been going on, and could I answer his questions, which I did. He said·"Was that the reason why your marriage broke up?". And I said "Well, there were three of us in this marriage and the pressure of the media was another factor. So the two together were very difficult. But although I still love your Papa I couldn't live under the same roof as him, and likewise with him".'

William, she said, is a 'deep thinker, and we won't know for a few years how it's gone in. But I put it in gently, without resentment or anger.'

The Charles documentary was watched by an estimated 15 million people, intent on hearing his views on his life, his loves, his future. But – by accident or design – it was Diana who walked away with all the best picture space in the next day's papers.

Fulfilling a long-standing engagement, she was filmed and photographed arriving at the Serpentine Gallery in London wearing a revealing and daring black evening dress.

It was, said author Andrew Morton, 'a flirty little number' and 'She could not have made a more appropriate choice, its style shouting the message "Whatever Charles may do, I'm having a ball."'

The Queen of People's Hearts

"*I think the biggest disease this world suffers from in this day and age is the disease of people feeling unloved, and I know that I can give love for a minute, for half an hour, for a day, for a month, but I can give. I'm very happy to do that and I want to do that.*"

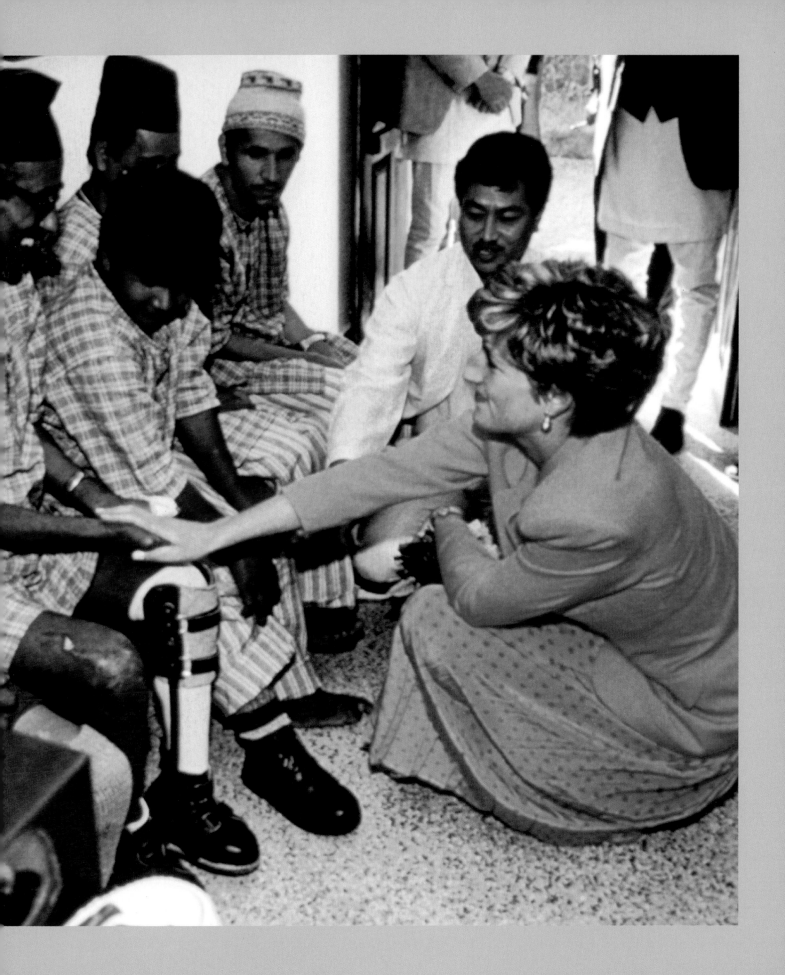

The woman within shone through the clothes she wore

Diana may have become famous through her marriage to a future King of England, but it was her leaving of the British royal family that allowed her, as she said, to do her own thing, and in doing so to become an international icon of fashion and a celebrity with massive popular appeal.

Her break with Charles freed her from the staid conformity of tradition in all directions, from the way things are done and said and the 'proper' form 'one' follows to the often frightful frumpery 'one' wears.

And her icon status – comparable now, the more excitable say, to the likes of Presley and Peron and Monroe – was never more obvious than at the memorial service for the designer Versace in Milan, just a month before Diana herself died a shocking death.

The great and the good and the glitzy of the world were there to see and be seen. But it was that once painfully shy English kindergarten assistant they all wanted to see as she gently soothed the sobbing singer Elton John.

'Members of the Press', reported the *London Evening Standard's* Mimi Spencer, 'stood silently behind a barrier at the service, but each fashion editor and every photographer shuffled as far forward as possible, desperate to get a glimpse of Diana – to view her glossy blonde hair, measure up her sleek black suit, gauge her high-heeled court shoes.

'Other members of the congregation were more blatant still, ignoring the high-Catholic Mass to crane their necks and grab sight of the Princess in their midst. Everyone wanted a look, at Versace's memorial and everywhere and anywhere she went.'

Why? 'Diana possessed that provocative

Right and inset: The young and fashion-naive Diana in 1982. The classic frills and trademark fringe are clearly evident.

Above: Diana's first fashion statement, on the occasion of her meeting Princess Grace of Monaco in 1980. This stunning black dress was made by David and Elizabeth Emanuel.

alchemy of good looks, fame and an increasingly honed sense of style that made her an irresistible attraction to the style-hungry hordes across the globe.'

She had travelled a hundred and more fashion miles from the time the nation, and the globe, first saw her, as a smart and sensible teenage 'Sloane Ranger' in frumpy 'pie-crust' frills, to the smooth and sophisticated woman of the world in that daring 'I'll show 'em' black number at the Serpentine Gallery.

Within weeks of her Sloaney phase she was walking down the aisle in that Emanuel 'fairy-tale princess' wedding dress – the first of her many strong links with British designers – and

> *"No other woman had the power to generate so many front pages across the world for the sake of one navy dress."*

soon after brides around the world were wondering if they could match it, without quite so many metres of train.

From there she went on to the peak – to the cover of British *Vogue*, as well as a million other magazine covers, to the charity sale of her dresses at Christie's in New York and her position as the most important public clothes-horse for British designers like Elizabeth Emanuel, Zandra Rhodes, Bruce Oldfield and Catherine Walker.

Foreign designers also courted her – among them Gianni Versace and Bernard Arnault, owner of the luxury goods group LVMH, who talked her into wearing that first dress for Christian Dior by John Galliano in 1996.

'No other woman had the power to generate so many front pages across the world for the sake of one navy dress', says Tasmin Blanchard, Fashion Editor of *The Independent*. 'She could not do anything to her appearance

Above: Bruce Oldfield, one of Diana's favourite designers, created the pleated gold lamé dress she wore in Melbourne in 1985.

without comment from the newspapers. She was every designer's dream.'

And the secret of that elusive appeal? 'Diana's style was a natural one. She was just as at home in a couture ball gown at a state ceremony as she was in her gym kit, or with windswept hair and bullet-proof waistcoat on the minefields of Angola.

'It was precisely the fact that she was a woman trying to control her own life, acknowledging her position as a role model to other women, while not being afraid to wear a one-shoulder dress or a skirt split high up the thigh that made Diana so alluring. Nobody was pulling her strings, either in her choice of dress or the way she chose to lead her life.'

She was doing her own thing, as she did with that stunning creation she wore on the night of Prince Charles' confession to Jonathan Dimbleby, when she had a date at London's Serpentine Gallery.

'She was irritated', Andrew Morton has reported, 'when the couturiers Valentino

Above: Having mistakenly left her tiara at home, Diana improvises by substituting Queen Mary's £2 million choker during a visit to Melbourne in 1985. Right: Diana during her 'Dynasty' period, wearing an outfit by Rifat Ozbek to a function in Madrid in 1987.

Right: Always the first to set new trends, Diana transforms formal menswear into the height of feminine chic during a charity visit to Wembley in 1988.

Whatever the occasion or clothes she wore, Diana effortlessly personified the height of elegance. The Catherine Walker dress and magnificent jewellery (above left) contrast with the more casual, sleek pencil skirt (above right) worn in Thailand in 1988.

Above: At Ascot in 1988 as at every other event she attended Diana was always the centre of attention.

Far right: Diana's style sold more swimsuits than any supermodel has ever endorsed. Here she is wearing a bikini by Jantzen, on the Caribbean island of Nevis in 1993.

prematurely announced that she would be wearing one of their dresses for the function. Once again, determined to make the point that she was in charge of her life, she left it in the wardrobe and donned a flirty number by Christina Stambolian.' And made, as everyone saw, a sensational entrance.

She had style, and Diana's style, says Tasmin Blanchard, 'was at its best when, as for those *Vanity Fair* pictures, she was at her

> **"Diana's true style only began to come into its own over the past four years, since the separation from Charles."**

most relaxed, natural and dressed down. She suited nothing better than a pair of jeans and a crisp white shirt.

'How thoroughly modern of her to own about 30 pairs of jeans – Rifat Ozbek, Armani and Versace, as well as good old traditional Levi's, were among the labels on the waistbands.

'Diana's true style only began to come into its own over the past four years, since the separation from Charles. She asserted her independence by moving away from frills and flounces and into a cleaner, sharper, more contemporary way of dressing.

'However, it is the woman within, rather than the clothes she wore, that will always shine through.'

Some, of course, would disagree. Like Vivienne Westwood, the designer renowned for kooky creations.

She protested a few years back: 'The princess isn't a trendsetter. She's someone

Above: The Queen of Style. Seen here at the British Fashion Awards in 1989, Diana looks stunning in an 'Elvis style' beaded gown by Catherine Walker.

ruled by the trends, which is sad because she's a stunning woman. I hate her shoes – those horrible little pumps that are neither one thing nor the other. It's as though her clothes are supposed to tell you she's both a feminist and sexy at the same time. It's a compromise and it doesn't work.'

Miss Westwood told *Woman and Home* magazine: 'Oh, I'd love to dress her. Perhaps one day she'll come to me. It would be great for her if she did. You'd see some results. I could make her the most stylish woman in the world.'

Diana achieved that title without help from Vivienne Westwood. And courtiers' hair might have curled at the prospect of her as couturier to Diana, as the fashion pundit Ollie Picton-Jones of *The Mirror* pointed out.

'They remember', she said, 'that when the

Below: Diana's off-duty casual wear regularly made headlines. On outings with the boys she would happily 'dress down' in sweater and slacks and still catch the eye.

Above: Diana auctioned off this dress along with seventy-eight others in a huge sale in 1997 which succeeded in raising millions of pounds for charity.

Above: A visit to Pakistan, 1996. Diana always made an effort to add a touch of local style to her outfits wherever she was in the world, and it was always appreciated by the people of the visiting country.

designer went to Buckingham Palace to collect her OBE, it was only too obvious that she had forgotten part of her outfit. Her knickers.'

Back in a more sensible world, Mimi Spence said: 'We were all, to varying degrees, obsessed with the cult of Diana.

'She provided unending and ample opportunities in the style press; she was our very own Jackie O, our Grace Kelly, whether appearing on the front cover of *Vogue*, on *Panorama* with heavily-kohled eyes, or at the Savoy Hotel for the 'courage and bravery awards', expertly dressed in a neat pink skirt suit and pale leather shoes.

'Diana fulfilled the role of 'princess' as no other British royal has ever done. The fashion world in America and on the Continent was as enamoured as we British, and the enormous public interest worldwide was a fillip for our own sense of style. On the global stage, she was a woman of whom we could be proud.

'As a style icon of the late 20th century, Diana will have no equal.'

Diana's styling in the mid 80s was sophisticated without necessarily being fussy. She is pictured (above) in Vienna in 1986, wearing a simple but elegant Catherine Walker dress, and (top) in a glamorous velvet boat-neck gown.
Catherine Walker was one of Diana's favourite designers, responsible for a vast array of different looks. The regal dress (left) was worn by Diana during her visit to Thailand in 1988.

Above: Diana's changing hairstyle was a major part of her appearance. She is pictured at the New York Fashion Awards wearing the slick-back look made famous by Catherine Walker.
Below: At the America's Cup Ball in 1986 in a Murray Arbeid bodice and red skirt.

Above: Every inch the fairytale princess, Diana shone in this dazzling sequined bodice and tiara during her tour of India in February 1992.

The high and low – she touched them all

But she was, of course, much more than a 'clothes horse'. She had become a much sought-after celebrity in her own right and moved among the film, theatre, dance, music and showbusiness set as though born to it.

In what she called her 'nest', her private sitting-room on the first floor of her Kensington Palace apartment, Diana proudly displayed silver-framed pictures of her boys, go-karting, at the controls of tanks and in school uni-form. But she also treasured photographs of herself dancing with film director Richard Attenborough and in the company of stars like Elton John and Liza Minelli.

In lonely moments, away from the limelight, she loved to curl up amid pillows embroidered with fun messages ('You have to kiss a lot of frogs before you find a Prince' said one) and listen to soothing choral and church music.

But her favourite CDs also included music from *Phantom of the Opera* and *Les Miserables*, Pavarotti – who she famously

Above: After two years 'in the job' Diana showed how well she had learned to cope with the demands of celebrity, moving at ease through an excited crowd during a tour of Canada in 1983.

Above: Despite her exalted status, Diana never lost her ability to relate to and charm ordinary people, such as these Chelsea Pensioners met in 1992.

Right: Diana in 1993 with business tycoon Richard Branson. Diana became friendly with Branson and his family and she and her sons spent some time holidaying on his private island in the Caribbean.

Below: Young or old – members of the public instinctively warmed to Diana and felt that she took a personal interest in their lives. Here she greets an elderly lady on a visit to Nottingham in 1992.

Above: The singer, and fellow tennis fan, Cliff Richard is introduced to the Princess at the Stella Artois Championship in London in 1993.

braved a British summer downpour to hear singing in London's Hyde Park in 1991 – and *Chariots of Fire* composer Vangelis.

Dance was her passion and she happily remembered partnering the best, most memorably John Travolta and then Wayne Sleep, with whom she took to the stage at the Royal Opera House in a high-kicking up-beat waltz as a surprise Christmas present for her husband of four years in 1985.

Years later, on the day her divorce from Charles was made final, it was no surprise that she spent it visiting the studios of the English National Ballet, a company of which she was patron – a cherished role for the woman whose childhood ambition was to be a ballerina and one she was determined to keep when she severed her links with almost 100 other organisations.

Another star friend was supermodel Cindy Crawford, whom Diana first met when she

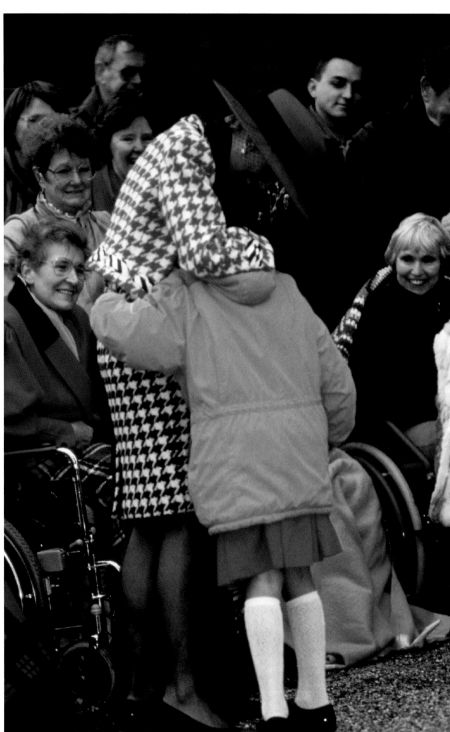

Above: A warm embrace for one of the crowd gathered outside at the christening in 1990 of Eugenie, the second daughter of the Duke and Duchess of York.
Left: With Nancy Reagan outside the White House during the tour of America in 1985.

invited her to Kensington Palace as a special treat for Prince William, who had a crush on her.

But life for the new single Diana was far from a round of fun and friendship. She had set out her aims in life in her famous *Panorama* television interview in November 1995, during which she admitted her adultery with former Life Guards officer James Hewitt.

Though divorce had not then been mentioned publicly, Diana admitted that she would never be Queen: 'I'd like to be a queen of people's hearts, in people's hearts', she said.

'But I don't see myself being Queen of this country. I don't think many people will want me to be Queen.'

By 'many people', she explained, she meant 'the Establishment that I married into, because they have decided that I'm a non-starter because I do things differently,

Above: Diana outshone even composer Paul McCartney and his wife Linda at a performance of his Liverpool Oratorio *in Lille in 1992.*

because I don't go by a rule book, because I lead from the heart, not the head. But someone's got to go out there and love people and show it...

'I think every strong woman in history has had to walk down a similar path, and I think it's the strength that causes the confusion and the fear.'

People asked, said Diana, 'Why is she strong? Where does she get it from? Where is she taking it? Where is she going to use it? Why do the public still support her?'

Whatever the answers to those questions, the simple fact was that the public did still support her – and Diana planned to use their support in her efforts to help those who needed it most.

Above: Diana could get on with all manner of people irrespective of creed or colour.
Right: With Sir Richard Attenborough at the opening of a centre for Disability and the Arts, 1997.

Above: Diana is introduced to singer and composer Elton John in May 1991 before a charity performance of Tango Argentino *which was held at the Aldwych Theatre, London to benefit the National Aids Trust, a charity of which Princess Diana was the Patron.*

Above: Diana breaks into a peal of laughter while being introduced to Jack Charlton and other members of the England 1966 World Cup-winning football team at an event held at Earl's Court in London to mark the 40th anniversary of the Queen's accession to the throne.

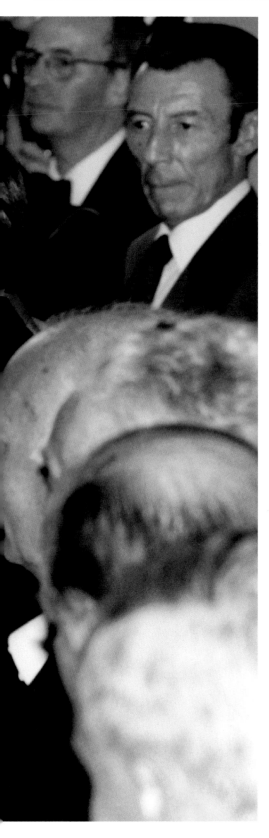

Right: Princess Diana comforted Elton John during the funeral of murdered fashion designer Gianni Versace in July 1997. By a tragic twist of fate, he was to sing at her funeral service just a few weeks later.

Left: A gallant tribute to a people's princess during a visit to Brazil in April 1991. Diana touched the hearts of people she met wherever she travelled across the globe.

Above and right: A star amongst stars – Diana meets Hollywood actor and director Clint Eastwood at a film première in 1993 and actress/singer Liza Minelli in 1991.

Fulfilling her mission to help the world

Diana's plan, she revealed, was to put the enormous worldwide fascination with her to good use: 'When I go abroad we've got 60 to 90 photographers, just from this country. So let's use it in a productive way.

'I've been in a privileged position for 15 years. I've got tremendous knowledge about people and how to communicate. I've learned that. I've got it, and I want to use it.'

She added: 'I think the biggest disease this world suffers from in this day and age is the disease of people feeling unloved, and I know that I can give love for a minute, for half an hour, for a day, for a month, but I can give. I'm very happy to do that and I want to do that.

'I think the British people need someone in public life to give affection, to make them feel important, to support them, to give them light in their dark tunnels. I see it as a possibly unique role.

'I've had difficulties, as everybody has witnessed over the years, but let's now use the knowledge I've gathered to help other people in distress.'

She set about her self-imposed task with steely determination – and became the most successful fund-raiser on the planet.

At one stage Diana was associated with some 150 charities, and was president or patron of more than 90, and when she severed links with all but six of them, officials estimated it would cost them a staggering total of £300 million. But she still lent her name and backing to many charitable causes and helped raise the profile of such issues as AIDS and landmine victims.

And hospital patients sometimes awoke in the small hours to find the 'Queen of Hearts', clad in jeans and baseball cap, at their bedside during her regular secret ward rounds to comfort the sick and the dying.

The 'special six' Diana concentrated on included the Leprosy Mission, to whom she made substantial personal donations as well as raising its profile. A fund-raising meal at Kensington Palace brought in £100,000.

There was her beloved English National Ballet, for whom a Diana event could raise £50,000 to £80,000 a time, and the Centrepoint charity for the homeless, to whom her patronage brought 'unquantifiable' funds and attention.

She was patron of the National AIDS Trust and helped put their work in front of the public, as well as raising many thousands of

Above: Many hands…a young helper assists Diana to plant a tree at a cancer treatment centre for children.

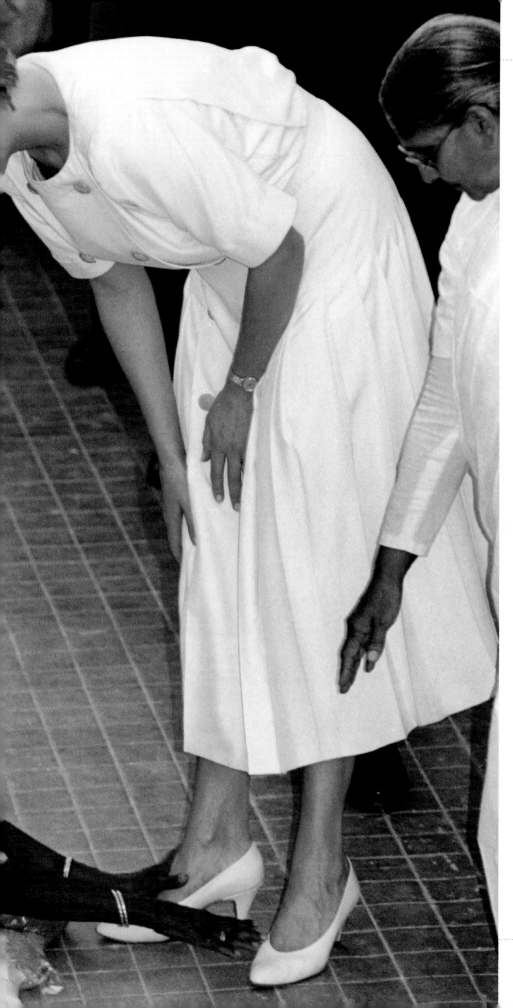

pounds to help them to do it. And as President of the Royal Marsden NHS Trust at the London cancer hospital she kept up a constant, keen interest in patients and research. One Diana trip to Chicago raised $800,000 for the hospital – and the auction of her clothes in New York brought in another £1 million.

Last, but not least in the six 'favourites', was London's Great Ormond Street Hospital for Children, of which Diana was Fund President. On many official or private visits to wards, she sought out the shyest child for

> *"I've had difficulties…but let's now use the knowledge I've gathered to help other people in distress."*

her special attention – and with Prince Charles she launched the Wishing Well appeal, which raised more than £50 million.

Children were her delight – friends said Diana always wanted a little girl – and she made a beeline for those she felt most needed her attention. One of them was eight-year-old Danielle Stephenson, from Southend-on-Sea, whose story dramatically illustrates Diana's concern.

When Danielle first met the princess, she had no idea of the identity of the special person who was to visit the Rose Ward of London's Royal Brompton Hospital, where she was lying ill with an irregular heartbeat.

Danielle remembers: 'A nurse told us someone very famous was coming and we tried to guess who it was. I thought it was going to be Alan Shearer.'

Left: Diana famously announced that it was her intention to reach out and touch people, to offer them love. And people wanted to reach out to her, as on this visit to Pakistan in 1996.

Above and left: In December 1995 Diana was presented with an award for her humanitarian
work. She is seen in company with the former US Secretary of State Dr Henry Kissinger.
Something of the strain of living in the public gaze is captured in these pictures.

It was, in fact, Diana, paying a private visit to the hospital to see a patient in another ward, and Danielle stood near the lifts with her friends to catch a glimpse of the VIP. But not for long. Within minutes of Diana appearing on the scene, she was sitting on Danielle's bed, both of them laughing at the antics of the stars in TV's *Absolutely Fabulous*.

And it was not a rare, one-off visit. 'The first time we met her', says Danielle, 'my friend Sophie shook her hand and said she had just been to the loo and hadn't washed her hands. Princess Di was really laughing.'

As Danielle clambered over her, Diana was obviously entranced, and promised to visit her again. 'We didn't really expect to see her again', says Danielle's mother, Denise. 'But she was as good as her word. She didn't come back just once, but again and again.

'One night Diana popped her head around the door of the ward and said she was sorry it was so late. But she asked if it was all right to come in for a moment to see us. It was as though she was putting us out by coming to visit Danielle.'

What, Danielle was asked, did they have in common? 'We used to talk about everything', she said. 'I told her about my guinea-pigs and she said she used to have guinea-pigs and hamsters. We talked about Ricky and Bianca in *EastEnders*, and I used to ask her about her boys and she'd tell me how they were.'

After an operation, Danielle left the hospital and it seemed her special friendship might be over. But they met again at the launch of the book *Heart of Britain*, a compilation of pictures taken by men, women and children throughout Britain to raise funds for the Royal Brompton's appeal to boost research into heart and lung disease.

Diana had written a foreword to the book, in which she said: 'Heart disease, the biggest killer in the western world today, still claims one in three lives, and many readers of this book may have lost family members and friends this way.

'I have been privileged to see for myself the miracles – at the very leading edge of medicine today – by the team of surgeons, doctors

and nurses at the Royal Brompton Hospital, whose dedication saves so many lives.'

She added: 'I have been profoundly impressed, too, to see how bravely patients cope, and have been particularly touched by the courage and trust shown by Britain's little people – our children. All need our compassion, our love and our support at what is often their darkest hour.'

Among them was her friend Danielle, and when they met again they hugged and talked as they had before. And the princess invited her and her mother to call at Kensington Palace whenever they had to come to the hospital for further treatment.

Danielle's mother says: 'I called her one day and she was really apologetic that she couldn't make it to the hospital. But she asked if we could possibly go round to see her. We were a little daunted going to the Palace, but as soon as she heard we were there she rushed down to meet us.

'She gave Danielle a cuddle and we were made to be totally at home. She got us cold drinks and we stayed for a chat.' And she gave them little presents – little posies of flowers and a pair of initialled chains for Danielle and her sister Natasha, who is seven.

The princess lent Danielle videos – of *Annie*, *Mask* and a Michael Jackson concert – and

Right: The importance of a hug – Diana comforts a baby during her visit to a hospital for cancer victims in Pakistan in 1996.

Above: Diana visited Nepal to see for herself the type of fieldwork in which the Red Cross, a charity close to heart, was involved.
Right: Visiting the National Children's Hospital in Tokyo in February 1995. Diana responded particularly warmly to little children.

once took her a cake. And on one occasion even offered to lend her mother some of her underwear.

Mrs Stephenson explained: 'Danielle had to go back into hospital at short notice and I was caught unprepared. My husband brought me an overnight bag, but forgot to pack any underwear. And when Diana came to see Danielle and I mentioned this point, she was wonderful.

'Diana said straight away that she would have brought something of hers to lend me. Then she insisted we bring laundry to her home, rather than taking it back to do in Southend.'

Danielle was back in hospital when she heard that her princess would visit her no

more. 'She is going to be an angel now, because God will look after her', she said. 'I want to take some flowers to her house. I want to get the biggest bunch I can find.'

As well as her often-unnoticed help at British hospitals, Diana also famously helped the work of Mother Theresa of Calcutta and Imran Khan, the former Pakistani cricket hero, with his charity cancer hospital. 'This world has few people like Diana', he said, 'who work so devotedly for the wellbeing of the poor, deprived and down-trodden.'

Recalling her visit to the hospital, where she was shown around by Imran and his wife Jemima, Diana said she was still deeply moved by the memory of a little blind boy she had cradled in her arms: 'A little sick boy

caught my eye. A solemn little boy with sad eyes and an emaciated body. And I couldn't look at anyone else but him.

'I don't know why, but I knew he was going to die. "Can I take him in my arms?", I said to his mother. She was full of smiles, delighted. We laughed, in a nice way, as she handed me the child. But then he begged me with his little anxious voice "Please don't mock me".

'I was disconcerted, but the mother explained that we were only talking. I hugged him very tight. The child died soon afterwards. I can remember his face, his suffering, his voice. I haven't forgotten.'

Television personality Esther Rantzen praised Diana's work for the Childline charity,

Above: Diana's willingness to touch and hug patients suffering from AIDS bore eloquent testimony to her compassion for the sick. As she explained, they needed such signs of affection more than most.
Left: Diana with Danielle, a patient at the Royal Brompton Hospital, with whom she struck up a long-term friendship.

and Nick Partridge, chief executive of the Terence Higgins Trust, said: 'Diana took the stigma away from AIDS. She was one of the first and most committed champions on this issue.'

But it was her most recent campaign, against landmines, which really engaged Diana's passions. 'What's to discuss', she demanded, 'when people are being blown up?'

When she flew to Angola, one of the world's most heavily-mined countries, to highlight the campaign, she finally believed she had achieved her stated aim – of linking the public's unending fascination with her to make a tangible difference to the lives of others.

'I hope', she told the Press pack who followed her, 'that by working together we shall focus world attention on this vital – but until now largely neglected – issue.'

Her visit was clouded in controversy when a Conservative minister branded her 'a loose cannon' and others accused her of being 'uninformed' about the landmines issue. But although Diana was initially

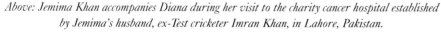

Above: Jemima Khan accompanies Diana during her visit to the charity cancer hospital established by Jemima's husband, ex-Test cricketer Imran Khan, in Lahore, Pakistan.

Above: 'She brings a little light to our lives' exclaimed President Robert Mugabe during Diana's visit to promote her charity work in Zimbabwe in 1993.

shocked and dismayed at the row that she had unwittingly stirred up, she refused to let it shake her determination to try to solve the horrific problem.

'All I am trying to do is help', she said. 'I saw the row at Westminster as merely a distraction. It meant things went off the rails for five minutes and went back on again. It's not helpful, things like that, but it does happen when a campaign is entwined in a political issue. I understand that.'

How, she was asked, had she got involved in the first place? 'A lot of information started landing on my desk about landmines, and I suppose the pictures were so horrific...that I felt perhaps if I could be part of a team to raise the profile around the world, it would help.'

Film director Lord Attenborough was a vital link, too: 'He invited me to the film premiere of *In Love and War*, which is raising money for the British Red Cross landmines appeal. So it seemed sensible to come out here to take some pictures to make the people sitting in their comfortable seats in Leicester Square understand where their money is going...'

Left and above: Diana's visit to Angola in January 1997 focused the world's attention on the problem of landmines and the sufferings of amputees injured by them. Despite some political rumblings of discontent at home, she insisted that 'All I'm trying to do is help'.

Above: Pictures of the Princess dressed in protective clothing in an Angolan minefield created huge public interest in the issue of landmines.
Right: In an interview with Le Monde *newspaper published only four days before she died, Diana explained 'I touch people. I think that everyone needs that. Placing a hand on a friend's face means making contact, tenderness.'*

She added: 'I didn't have any set agenda. I didn't know what to expect. I was open-minded about it, but I'm surprised at the level of injuries. The number of amputees is quite shocking.

'You read the statistics, but actually going into the centres and seeing them struggling to gain a life again after they have had something ripped off – that is shocking.'

Sometimes, Diana admitted, the scenes she saw were horrifying. 'But over the years I've learned to cope with it, because each person is an individual. Each person needs a bit of love. You don't think about yourself. You always take it home with you. I have lasting impressions of people struggling and they are very touching.'

Especially she remembered a little girl she had met in hospital: 'She had her intestines blown out. She's very, very, poorly, and I think just looking at her and thinking what was going on inside her head and heart was very disturbing.

'But she's just one statistic, and there are millions of landmines lying around. Someone has got to do something.'

That someone, she had decided, was herself – and, once she had committed herself to the cause, The Queen of Hearts was a very determined lady.

*"My heart is
full of grief
and pain.*
Lady Diana was the most
beautiful symbol of humanity
and love for all the world.*

A World in Mourning

*She touched my life in an
extraordinary way. I'll always
remember her with deep love
and joy."*

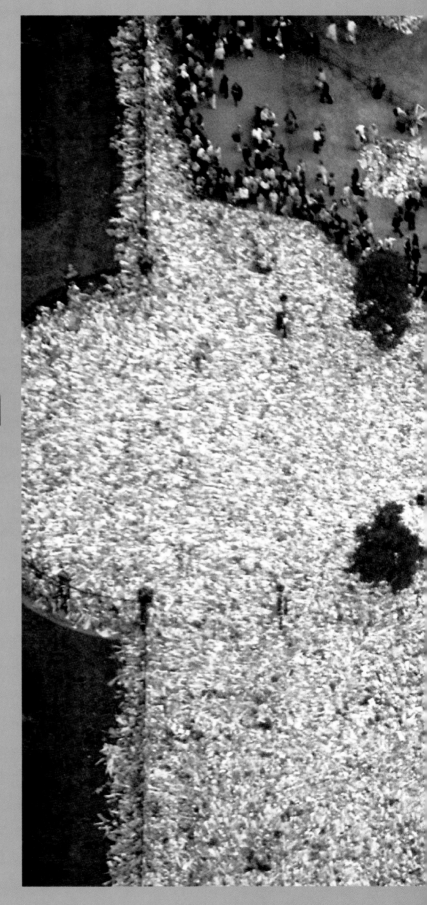

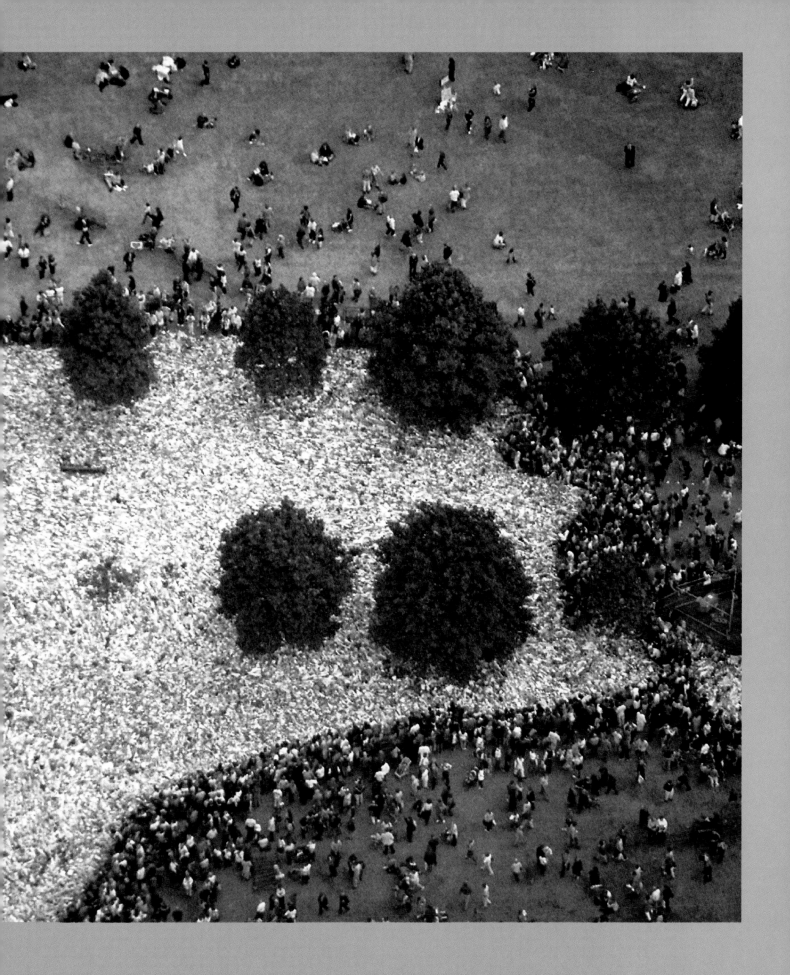

Diana finally found the love she longed for

It was a miserable Monday morning, a dull mid-December day in 1995, when the final acts in the marriage of Charles and Diana, which had once held so much hope and promise, were played out.

Diana put through a call to the Queen saying she felt it would be 'more comfortable' for everyone if she did not join the royal family for their Christmas at Sandringham. 'I'd have gone there in a BMW', she told a friend later, 'and come out in a coffin.'

That afternoon a handwritten letter from the Queen was delivered to Diana at Kensington

Above: Dodi Fayed. After their Mediterranean holiday in 1997, Diana confided to a friend that she felt newly loved.

Palace. It suggested that, for the sake of the children, Diana and Charles should be divorced sooner rather than later. A similar letter was delivered to Charles later that day.

Next morning Diana began discussions with Anthony Julius, a senior lawyer at Mishcon de Reya, whose senior partner Lord Mishcon had advised her during the separation.

Two days later the contents of the Queen's letter were leaked to the Press and picked up on television – and Diana saw the news on TV when she returned to Kensington Palace after taking Harry to the local cinema to see the James Bond film *Goldeneye*. She was devastated. 'How could they do this at Christmas?', she asked.

The divorce – in which Diana won a settlement estimated at £17 million but lost the right to the title Her Royal Highness – was announced in February the following year after much legal wrangling.

But, speaking of Prince Charles, Diana told a friend: 'What a lot of people don't realise is that we are actually very good friends, and I speak to him on the phone all the time. He even pops in here. I think a lot of people might be very surprised if they knew that.'

But in the following months, Diana began to lead an increasingly lonely and isolated life. 'I had so many dreams as a young girl', she said. 'I hoped for a husband to look after me. He would be a father figure to me, he would support me, encourage me, say "Well done" or "That wasn't good enough."

'I didn't get any of that. I couldn't believe it. I have learned so much over the last years. From now on I am going to own myself and be true to myself. I no longer want to live someone else's idea of what and who I should be. I am going to be me.'

The divorce became absolute in August, 1996, and the following night Diana was due at a Red Cross presentation in London. But

she cancelled at the last moment: 'I just can't go', she said. 'I'm so sorry.'

'People will be so sympathetic to me and nice. I will cry, and I don't want to do that because everyone will be so upset. All the coverage will be about me crying, and nothing will be said about the charity.'

Under the divorce agreement, she would be known as Diana, Princess of Wales, and that proved a sticking point until she asked Prince William about it. He told her: 'I really don't mind what you're called. You're Mummy.'

It was agreed that she should continue to live at Kensington Palace, to provide a

Left: Elegant as ever, Diana arrives for the London film première of In Love and War, *directed by her friend Lord Attenborough, on 12 February 1997.*

secure home for her sons, although she had to remove her office from St James' Palace. It suited Diana, who had never seriously considered going to live abroad.

'I think that in my place any sane person would have left long ago', she said. 'But I can't. I have my sons.'

Gradually, her self-confidence grew, especially as she felt she could now achieve her aim of helping others in her own, highly individual way. And partly, some now believe, because of her growing romance with Dodi Fayed, the film-producer son of controversial businessman Mohamed Al Fayed.

Some saw Dodi, a graduate of Sandhurst military academy and a former London officer for the United Arab Emirates, as a totally unsuitable partner for the mother of a future British king. He had a reputation as a handsome playboy with a love of fast cars and beautiful women. And he'd been married to American socialite Suzanne Gregard – although the 1987 marriage had lasted just eight months.

Others said the couple, who first met at a Windsor polo match some 10 years earlier, were perfectly suited and very much in love. Among them is Cindy Crawford, the supermodel who had become close to Diana.

She said she'd learned about the romance several months before it became public – in November 1996, when Diana had whisked her from Kensington Palace around to Harrods, owned by Dodi's father, even though it was long after the famous store's closing time.

As they stood in the dark, deserted store, all the lights were suddenly switched on, said Cindy – and Dodi Fayed came down an escalator. 'May I present Dodi?', Diana said. 'Here he is the boss – and also my boyfriend.'

Cindy asked if they would marry. 'It's too soon to say', Diana replied. 'Besides, I'm so happy I don't even have time to think about

Above: The flamboyant businessman Mohamed Al Fayed welcomes Princess Diana to Harrods for the launch of the charity book Heart of Britain, *October 1996.*

it.' But the model believes that Diana was 'truly happy' with Dodi. 'She had found in him the companion she had been searching for in her life. He and Diana were simply two people in love.'

Their romance became public when the sleek, relaxed princess was pictured with her sons, sunbathing and diving from Dodi's father's yacht in the Mediterranean. After returning the boys to Britain, Diana flew to France again to enjoy a further five-day holiday with Dodi on the yacht off Corsica and Sardinia.

From the yacht she telephoned Cindy

Crawford to confide her feelings to her: 'Dodi and I are enjoying the last days of our holiday. I'm immensely happy. I say that seriously, you know.

'For the first time in my life I can say I'm truly happy. Dodi is a fantastic man. He covers me with attention and with care. I feel newly loved.'

Next day, Diana, aged 36, was dead, killed with Dodi in the horrific midnight Paris car crash which stunned the world. And for countless millions, who had followed every twist and turn of her incredible life story, the fairytale was indeed over.

Diana – the silent homecoming

Above: The Ritz Hotel in Paris, the fateful venue for Diana and Dodi's final dinner.

Within hours of Diana's death, tributes were pouring in from princes and presidents and from the ordinary people around the world to whom Diana would always be the People's Princess.

And what vividly characterised their words, and set them apart from the usual stereotyped sayings that mark the passing of the great and the good, was their obvious warmth and honesty and sincere expressions of genuine and deeply heartfelt grief.

Instead of the often-exaggerated and ritual messages of sympathy, the tributes to Diana were direct and personal – partly because she was known and liked by many of the world and church leaders, stars and celebrities who voiced them.

But largely because of what she was to them, and many millions of 'ordinary' people who had never even met her – a concerned and committed woman who sincerely wanted to help those who needed it most.

Above: Sunday August 31, 1997 – the body of Princess Diana is borne across the silent tarmac of RAF Northolt airfield by pall bearers from the Queen's Colour Squadron. Prince Charles had accompanied Diana's sisters, Lady Jane Fellowes and Lady Sarah McCorquodale, on the doleful journey home.

Above: The news of Diana's death triggered the most extraordinary outpouring of public grief. Personal messages and floral tributes are here seen on the gates of Kensington Palace.

TONY BLAIR led the British tributes. Speaking with obvious emotion before he attended a church service in his Sedgefield constituency, he declared: 'I feel like everyone else in this country today. I am absolutely devastated.'

His voice trembling, the Prime Minister said Britons would never forget the Princess who had brought joy and comfort to so many people all over the world.

'They liked her. They loved her. They regarded her as one of the people. She was the people's princess and that's how she will stay, how she will remain, in our hearts and in our memories forever.

'Our thoughts and prayers are with Princess Diana's family, particularly her two sons. Our heart goes out to them. We are today a nation in a state of mourning, in grief that is so deeply painful for us. She touched the lives of so many in Britain and throughout the world.'

Mr Blair, who had met the princess just a few weeks earlier – and who later flew south to be present when Prince Charles and Diana's sisters brought her body back to Britain aboard the plane from Paris – added: 'She seemed full of happiness, full of life, and she was great fun to be with.

'She was an unusual but a really warm character and personally I shall remember her with great affection. I think the whole country will remember her with the deepest affection and love, and this is why our grief is so deep today.'

Above: A sea of flowers laps against the walls of Kensington Palace. Crowds of people waited for many long hours to sign the books of condolence (right).

Above: Diana's final resting place was to be in the grounds of Althorp House on the Althorp estate in Northamptonshire. Here again floral tributes to the Princess abounded.

Above: Diana's magical way with young children was reflected in the personal and deeply touching messages that they addressed to her. This young girl pauses in prayer outside Buckingham Palace.

FRANCES SHAND KYDD, Diana's mother, who lives on the Isle of Seil, near Oban on the west coast of Scotland, thanked everyone for their prayers, flowers and letters and added: *'I thank God for the gift of Diana and for all her loving and giving. I give her back to Him with my love, pride and admiration to rest in peace.'*

RAINE, COMPTESSE DE CHAMBRUN, Diana's stepmother, spoke of *'her capacity for love, her willingness to go anywhere to help anyone in need. I will always remember her tremendous sense of fun and her wonderful gift of friendship.'*

PRESIDENT CLINTON said: *'Hillary and I knew Princess Diana and we were very fond of her. We are profoundly saddened by this tragic event. We liked her very much. We admired her for her work for children, for people with AIDS, for the cause of ending the scourge of landmines in the world and for her love for her children, William and Harry. I know this is a very difficult time for millions in the United Kingdom, who are deeply shocked and grieving, and the American people send their condolences to all of them.'*

KOFI ANNAN, the UN Secretary-General, praised Diana's *'unflinching commitment to the cause of banning landmines'* and added: *'The tragedy has robbed the world of a consistent and committed voice for the improvement of the lives of suffering children worldwide.'*

*Above: Floral tributes laid at the doors of
the British Embassy in Washington, D.C.
Below: The world cried for Diana, in Los
Angeles just as in London.*

*Above: Public expressions of grief were not confined to Britain. Candles of remembrance were lit
and bouquets of flowers left outside the British Consulate in New York.*

LIONEL JOSPIN, the French Prime Minister, said: *'It was profoundly sad that this beautiful young woman, loved by the people, and whose every act and gesture was scrutinised, should end her life tragically in France, in Paris'.*

NELSON MANDELA, the South African President, said: *'I vividly recall our meeting when she visited South Africa last year and her burning desire to assist HIV-positive children in Africa. She was undoubtedly one of the best ambassadors of Great Britain.'*

IMRAN KHAN said: *'There was hardly any non-Muslim who worked in a non-Muslim country with as much dedication as Diana demonstrated for the sick and poor in Pakistan'.*

HELMUT KOHL, the German Chancellor, said: *'Many people in Germany loved her because of her openness and humanitarian engagement'.*

Above: The initial shock at the news of Diana's death gave way to anger at the role played by the paparazzi. The grafitti on the bridge over the fatal underpass branded them murderers.

Above: Nelson Mandela praised her, and on the walls of one building in Johannesburg, Jason Askew painted this mural as a graphic tribute to the love that South Africa felt for her.

From Pakistan (above) to Bosnia (below) the sentiments were the same.

JOHN HOWARD, the Australian Prime Minister, expressed the shock and sadness of all his people: *'The death, in such tragic circumstances, has ended at a young age, the life of a person who held a particular fascination for many people around the world'.*

BINYAMIN NETANYAHU, the Israeli Premier, said: *'The princess was a woman of grace, beauty and charm. She represented Britain with nobility and warmth, and she captured the imagination of millions throughout the world.'*

JASMINKO BJELIC, a 23-year-old landmine victim who met Diana on her visit to Bosnia a month before her death, said: *'I feel terrible. She was our friend.'*

THE DUCHESS OF YORK said she had lost *'a sister and a best friend...there are no words strong enough to describe the pain. The world has lost the most compassionate of humanitarians and someone so special, whose presence can never be replaced.'*

CARDINAL BASIL HUME, leader of the Roman Catholic Church in England and Wales, said: *'My deepest sympathy goes out to all the royal family and particularly to her two sons, to whom she was devoted'.*

Below: Sites that bore Diana's name seemed to act as magnets for the grieving millions. This theatre in Toronto, Canada – the Princess of Wales – was piled high with floral tributes.

Above and far left: Headlines around the world told the same sad tale.

GEORGE CAREY, the Archbishop of Canterbury, said: *'She seized the imagination of young and old alike. This beautiful woman was also a very vulnerable human being, and out of that came lots of strength, her passion and her commitment to people.*

'The world has lost a vibrant, lovely young person. The word passion seems to sum her up – commitment to issues, to causes.'

ROSA MONCKTON, Diana's close friend, who had recently been on holiday with her, said: *'She did everything from the heart. Her heart ruled her head, which is why, I think, she was so often misunderstood. As a friend she was steadfast and loyal, and whenever I had any setback in my life she was immediately there and would drop everything.'*

ELTON JOHN, the singer whom Diana befriended, said: *'This is the most tragic and senseless death. The world has lost one of its most compassionate humanitarians and I have lost a special friend.'*

BORIS YELTSIN, the Russian President, said he was *'deeply shocked...the princess was well known and loved by the Russian people'*.

JOHN MAJOR, the former British Premier, said: *'She was an icon of our age and will leave an imperishable memory in the minds of millions'*.

LUCIANO PAVAROTTI, one of Diana's favourite singers, said: *'My heart is full of grief and pain. Lady Diana was the most beautiful symbol of humanity and love for all the world. She touched my life in an extraordinary way. I'll always remember her with deep love and joy.'*

BARONESS THATCHER, the former British Prime Minister, said: *'With her tragic death a beacon of light has been extinguished. Her good works brought hope to so many of those in need throughout the world.'*

Those were the famous people. But from all corners of Britain and the world there were ordinary people with remarkable stories to tell of Diana's dedication and love for them.

EMMA MAY, 16, from Copthorne in West Sussex, was born with Turner's Syndrome which stunted her growth and she had heart and kidney problems throughout her childhood. But Diana gave her the courage to go on.

She said: *'When I was 10 I won a bravery award for children who triumphed over adversity. The princess presented it to me and made me promise to keep in touch with her and let her know how I was getting on.'*

The promise led to a lengthy correspondence between Emma and Diana: *'She said how lovely it was to hear from me and was obviously really interested in my progress'*.

Emma organised a string of charity events to raise £30,000 for an operation. *'When I told Diana about the fund-raising, she wrote back with a contribution. She told me never to tell how much it was, but I can say her generosity was a big, big, help.'*

DEAN WOODWARD, 30, from Nottingham, was in intensive care in a hospital in the city after a car accident, when Prince Charles was brought in for treatment to an arm injury after a polo fall.

When Diana visited her then-husband and saw Dean's mother crying in a corridor, she asked to see him – and went back to see him four or five times during his six weeks in hospital.

She telephoned constantly to see how he was and even visited the family when Dean came out of hospital. Afterwards she kept in touch with them by letter, the last one only two months before she died.

Mrs Woodward said: *'We felt so privileged that someone so high up would come to see ordinary people like us'*.

VICTORIA HEMPHILL, 14, from County Londonderry in Northern Ireland, underwent a heart transplant, but had to be readmitted to Harefield Hospital in Middlesex when her body rejected the new heart.

Diana was asked by nurses if she would visit Victoria and she saw her several times. *'She was always bright and chirpy',* says Victoria, *'and afterwards I felt much better'*.

The princess and the patient talked of everything – her holidays, her trips abroad to spotlight the landmines issue, and her sons: *'She said she used to do extra little things for Harry because William would be King and she felt sorry for Harry because he wasn't going to be'*.

Diana brought gifts, too – a signed photograph of herself with her sons, flowers and fashion magazines – and asked Victoria to telephone her whenever she wanted. *'But I never did…I am so sad that I will not see her again. She was a real friend to me.'*

Left: Tears at Buckingham Palace and (top) a message of love outside Kensington Palace.

A simple message of love from a special friend

MOTHER TERESA said Diana, who'd become her friend, was devoted to the poor. *'All the sisters and I are praying for her and all the members of her family to know God's speed and peace and comfort in this moment.'*

Just five days later the Nobel-prize-winning nun, who dedicated her life to caring for the destitute and dying, was herself dead – of a heart attack at the age of 87, in the Calcutta mission she founded. The 'Saint of the Gutters' left just two saris, and the bucket she used to wash in.

The Queen pays tribute

The last major tribute to Diana – on the eve of her funeral – came from the Queen, making her first live broadcast in 38 years, following public criticism of her family's apparent indifference to the massive wave of public grief.

In the most remarkable and personal message of her reign, her broadcast was an open appeal for understanding, and a clear declaration that Diana's contribution to the monarchy would not only always be remembered but enhanced.

She began: *'Since last Sunday's dreadful news, we have seen throughout Britain and the world, an overwhelming expression of sadness at Diana's death. We have all been trying in our different ways to cope.*

'It is not easy to express a sense of loss, since the initial shock is often succeeded by a mixture of other feelings – disbelief, incomprehension, anger, and concern for those who remain.

'We have all felt all those emotions in these last few days. So what I say to you now, as your Queen and as a grandmother, I say from the heart.

'First, I want to pay tribute to Diana myself. She was an exceptional and gifted human being. In good times and bad, she never lost her capacity to smile and laugh, nor to inspire others with her warmth and kindness.

'I admired and respected her – for her energy and commitment to others, and especially for her devotion to her two boys.' The Queen, speaking with composure but with visible emotion, went on: *'This week at Balmoral, we have all been trying to help William and Harry to come to terms with the devastating loss that they and the rest of us have suffered.*

'No-one who knew Diana will ever forget her. Millions of others who never met her, but felt they knew her, will remember her. I for one believe that there are lessons to be drawn from her life and from the extraordinary and moving reaction to her

death. I share in your determination to cherish her memory.'

The Queen, grey haired now and dressed in black, continued: *'This is also an opportunity for me, on behalf of my family and especially Prince Charles and William and Harry, to thank all of you who have brought flowers, sent messages, and paid your respects in so many ways to a remarkable person.*

Above: The Queen and Prince Philip inspect the floral tributes and messages of love piled high outside the gates of Buckingham Palace.

'These acts of kindness have been a huge source of help and comfort.'

Speaking in the Chinese Room on the first floor of Buckingham Palace, against the scene outside packed with people and oceans of flowers, the Queen said: *'Our thoughts are also with Diana's family and the families of those who died with her.*

'I know they, too, have drawn strength from what has happened since last weekend as they seek to heal their sorrow and then to face the future without a loved one.'

The Queen ended: *'I hope that tomorrow we can all, wherever we are, join in expressing our grief at Diana's loss, and gratitude for her all-too-short life. It is a chance to show to the whole world the British nation united in grief and respect.*

'May those who died rest in peace and may we, each and every one us, thank God for someone who made many, many people happy.'

The Journey Home

"Goodbye England's rose,
From a country lost without
*   your soul,*
Who'll miss the wings of your
*   compassion,*
More than you'll ever know."

A nation united in its grief

The September sun came early that mournful morning, breaking gently through the thick old curtains of palaces and striking harshly at the people who'd slept in the parks and on the pavements of the ancient capital, where the fragrance of vast oceans of flowers filled the air.

The tens of thousands and more who had camped out overnight awoke to find the streets of London packed with crowds bigger than any since V-E Day in 1945 – up to two million was one estimate – and they were but a tiny fraction of those who watched the last sad farewell to Diana, the people's princess, on television: some 25 million, nearly half the population, in Britain and an extraordinary 2.5 billion throughout the world she had enchanted.

'But you really have to be here' said the Leeds pensioner who'd braved the chilly night outside Westminster Abbey with her husband (and 2,000 others), 'to feel the emotion and love that's all around. You can't get that on TV, can you? And that's what Diana was really all about – love.'

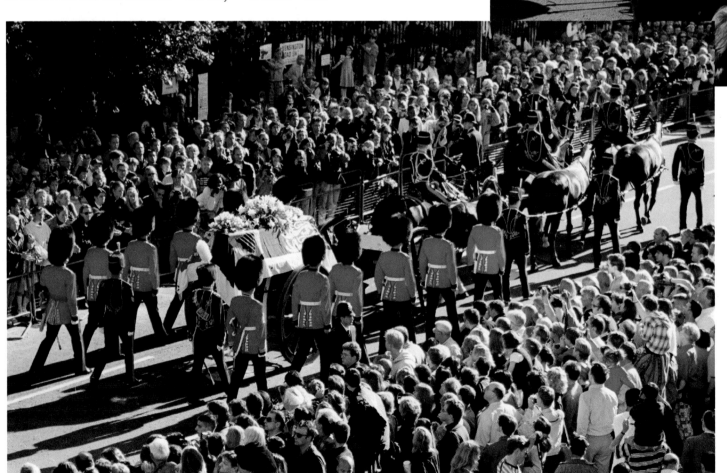

Above: The gun carriage bearing Diana's coffin from Kensington Palace to the Abbey begins its journey from Kensington Palace to Westminster Abbey.

Above: A wreath of white roses bearing a poignant message adorns Diana's coffin.

A historic and doleful sight: the Union flag flies at half mast (inset right) over Buckingham Palace (above) as the carriage, drawn by three pairs of horses, nears the Abbey. Inset, above right: The Queen and Princess Margaret watch as the cortege passes the Palace.

Hers was a simple but eloquent tribute shared by many waiting in London's flower-strewn streets, or in homes across the globe, for the start of a day they would remember all their lives.

It began as the Abbey's Tenor Bell began to toll, as it would every sad minute of Diana's slow journey to the service, through streets she knew so well, on what had been called 'a unique occasion for a unique person'.

At 9.08am, she left her Kensington Palace home for the last time, her coffin resting on a gun carriage drawn by three pairs of horses from The King's Troop, Royal Horse Artillery. The coffin, draped in the Royal Standard and flanked on foot by 12 members of the Welsh Guards, held three all-white wreaths, of lilies, tulips and roses, from the Spencer family and Diana's sons William and Harry, one marked simply and sadly 'Mummy'.

As the carriage moved slowly away from the private entrance of the Palace, people in the crowds – four and six and even 15 and 20 deep in places along the route – held their children up to catch the historic moments, and reacted in their own individual ways.

Many wept openly, unashamed to show their sorrow, or wailed loudly and eerily – a terrible keening. Others broke the Saturday morning silence as they applauded – the only way they could think to express their sorrow at that precious moment they would treasure for all time.

Some threw flowers into the path of the carriage, or hugged each other for comfort or shouted or murmured their farewells: 'God bless you' or 'We love you' or just 'Goodbye, Di'.

Most, though, simply stood in silence, heads bowed or looking straight ahead, alone with their thoughts and prayers for the woman they'd never known but who had

Diana's beloved sons follow her on the last stage of the journey to the Abbey.

Above: Some were silent, some wept – but all were united in their grief.

touched their lives and those of so many others so profoundly.

Slowly the cortege travelled on into Hyde Park, near the Royal Albert Hall, its entrance draped in black, in stark contrast to the many glittering occasions when Diana had been its star attraction.

At Hyde Park Corner a single red, heart-shaped balloon rose into the clear skies, and a banner strung to railings remarked: 'Diana – an English flower plucked away too soon...' Another, elsewhere, proclaimed: 'No-one can hurt you now ...feel the love'.

Yet another, daringly hoisted on the gates of Buckingham Palace itself, said: 'Diana of Love'.

Love, and lots of it, was what the people wanted to be the dominant theme of this dreadul day.

At the Palace there was a first break with tradition when the Queen led her family through the gates and stood outside on the pavement to pay her respects to the woman she'd told her subjects the previous evening was 'an exceptional and gifted human being'.

Close to the mountains of flowers laid during the week, the Queen waited quietly with

Princes Andrew and Edward, the Princess Royal and Princess Margaret, the Duchess of York and Princesses Beatrice and Eugenie, the Duke and Duchess of Kent and Lord Linley.

As the cortege reached the Palace – on time at 10.17am precisely – the monarch bowed her head sharply and briefly.

Then, as the Queen left by car for Westminster Abbey, came another remarkable break with tradition: Britain's national Union flag rose above the Palace for the first

Above: Head bent in grief, Prince William follows Diana's standard-draped coffin.

Above: Flanked by twelve members of the Welsh Guards, the carriage progresses down the Mall, nearing the end of its 107-minute journey.

From left: Hillary Clinton; the Duchess of York; Frances Shand Kydd, Diana's mother; and Tony and Cherie Blair.

Above: Approaching the eleventh hour, the cortege ended its four-mile journey at the flower-strewn entrance to Westminster Abbey.

time ever, before it was lowered to half-mast.

It meant the royal family, reacting to the people's unprecedented outpouring of sadness, was tearing up the protocol rulebook to show its support for that mood.

Until then only the Royal Standard had flown over the Palace to show that the Queen was in residence – and has never been flown at half mast, because it is a symbol of the continuity of the monarchy.

But the Queen ordered a change in the face of mounting public anger that for most of the week only the Palace's flagpole remained bare, in telling contrast to Union flags throughout the rest of the nation.

And her move brought instant public approval: as the flag was hoisted and then lowered to half mast over the Palace, the crowds outside burst into applause.

At St James's Palace, Princes William and Harry, with their father, waited to fall in behind their mother's coffin, with Prince Philip and Diana's brother, Earl Spencer, joining them as the chief mourners.

For the boys – particularly William, who would keep his head bowed for most of the morning – it was a daunting ordeal. But for William there were murmured words of help and comfort from Philip, and Earl Spencer – the emotional strain of the occasion clearly showing on his own face – put an encouraging arm around Harry.

As these five main mourners walked in perfect step behind the coffin, they were followed by 500 representatives of Diana's favourite

Above: Walking completely unaided, the Queen Mother accompanied the Queen into the Abbey before the entrance of the coffin and its five followers. Inside, a 2,000-strong congregation waited to show its love and respect.

Above: Earl Spencer's moving speech drew unprecedented applause from the congregation.

charities – a moving procession which included children in pushchairs and invalids in wheelchairs.

By the time they neared the final stretch on the 107-minute journey, the Queen Mother was being driven from Clarence House to the Abbey, already filled with a 2,000-strong congregation of family and friends, politicians and celebrities from the worlds of the arts and showbusiness.

Elton John, who was to sing his personal and poignant tribute to Diana, had been among the first to arrive, along with fellow pop-star George Michael. Then came mourners equally familiar to so many: Tony Blair and his wife Cherie, and Hillary Clinton, representing the President and all America, where informal floral shrines to Diana had appeared in almost every major city.

There were Diana's mother Frances Shand Kydd, and Raine Spencer. And the weary, careworn figure of Mohamed Al Fayed, mourning, too, for his beloved son Dodi, killed with Diana in that awful, senseless Paris car crash that seemed now to have happened many months and not just a few days ago.

His head held high, but with red eyes betraying his emotion, he walked briskly through the Abbey to take his place with his wife Heini.

Above: The scene in Hyde Park, where giant video screens allowed the huge crowd of mourners, many weeping unashamedly, to share in the events within the Abbey.

11am into the Abbey itself and to the blue-and-gold altar, where it was guarded by four tall candles during the service.

Its highlight, if it could be called such a thing on this sombre day, was the address by Earl Spencer, a statement of passion and love and anguish and sorrow for his lost sister, delivered in a quaking voice by a man whose grief was raw and tangible.

'Diana', he said, 'was the very essence of compassion, of duty, of style, of beauty.'

Then came his second attack on the media within a week – a fierce condemnation of those who had made his sister – named after the goddess of hunting – into 'the most hunted person of the modern age'.

'I don't think', he said, 'she ever understood why her genuinely good intentions were sneered at by the media, why there appeared to be a permanent quest on their behalf to bring her down'.

As he finished, there was the most extraordinary reaction. First several people listening to the service on loudspeakers outside

Left: A mourner's lighted candle echoes the words of Elton John's (above) own musical tribute to his much-loved friend.

From the world of politics came the French President's wife Madame Chirac, former Prime Ministers Margaret Thatcher and Sir Edward Heath, Foreign Secretary Robin Cook, Deputy Premier John Prescott, Opposition leader William Hague and Liberal Democrat leader Paddy Ashdown.

There, too, were Lord Steel, Henry Kissinger, Winston Churchill, Virginia Bottomley, Lord Callaghan and his daughter Baroness Jay, Lord Irving of Lairg, Cabinet Secretary Sir Robin Butler and Commons Speaker Betty Boothroyd.

From among Diana's music-world friends were her 'Lady in Red' favourite Chris de Burgh, Luciano Pavarotti, Sir Cliff Richard, Brian May, Diana Ross and Sting. From the film world were Lord Attenborough, Tom Cruise and Nicole Kidman, Tom Hanks, Steven Spielberg and Tom Conti, and from fashion Bruce Oldfield and the Emanuels, Karl Lagerfeld and Donatella Versace.

There were many more household names: Sir David Frost, Richard Branson, Imran Khan and his wife Jemima, Earl Snowdon, Clive James, Ruby Wax, Martin Bell. From the Church came former Archbishop of Canterbury Robert Runcie and the Roman Catholic leader Cardinal Basil Hume.

At two minutes to 11, the Welsh Guards hoisted the coffin on to their shoulders and carried it past the two young princes to the West Door of the Abbey – and at precisely

began to clap. Soon, the whole crowd took up the applause. And as the sound filtered through into the Abbey, the entire congregation joined in – an unheard-of thing at such a sombre and important English service.

Prince William and his brother joined in the applause and so, more discreetly – one hand clapping on his knee – did their father. But Charles was visibly moved by the music – the "Libera Me" from Verdi's *Requiem*, and favourite Diana hymns *The King of Love My Shepherd Is* and *I Vow to Thee My Country* – and by a short, telling, reading from Diana's sister, Lady Jane Fellowes: 'Time is too slow for those who wait, too swift for those who fear, too long for those who grieve, too short for those who rejoice. But for those who love, time is eternity'.

Charles glanced often at his boys, giving sidelong glances of support as they faced this most awful of public trials – the 12-year-old Harry gazing straight ahead at his mother's coffin, but his elder brother keeping his head bowed, his hand covering his face and occasionally wiping away the inevitable tear.

Both boys wept, though, and their father was close to it, when Elton John sat at a piano in the hushed Abbey to sing his most moving song, *Candle in the Wind*, with new lyrics especially composed for his good and

much-missed friend Diana.

He'd originally written it, with lyricist Bernie Taupin, as a tribute to Marilyn Monroe. But for this very special performance, requested by Diana's family and personally sanctioned by the Queen herself, he wrote poignant new lines to summarise in song the nation's grief:

Loveliness we've lost;
These empty days without
*   your smile.*
This torch we'll always carry
For our nation's golden child.

There were many other memorable moments – a reading by the princess' other sister, Lady Sarah McCorquodale: *If I should die and leave you here awhile/ Be not like others, sore undone, who keep/ Long vigils by the silent dust, and weep.*

There was Tony Blair reading, with evident emotion, from 1 Corinthians 13 ('And now abideth faith, hope, love, these three; but the greatest of these is love')… the haunting hymn *Cwm Rhondda*… the solemn, but beautiful, music of British composer John Tavener, with Horatio's farewell to Hamlet: 'Goodnight sweet prince, may flights of angels sing thee to thy rest'.

Yet as the years pass and memories of the service begin to fade, it will be that Elton John song, written many years ago for a Hollywood screen star and given new words and significance in 1997, that will linger on and keep Diana's life and tragic death fresh and firmly in our minds:

Above: Crowds of local people line the route as the procession nears Althorp.

Above: The final homecoming – Diana's hearse at the entrance to Althorp and its floral tribute.

Goodbye England's rose,
From a country lost without your soul,
Who'll miss the wings of your compassion,
More than you'll ever know.

As it all ended, the cortege was carried out and halted at the west end of the Abbey for a minute's silence, observed nationwide.

The half-muffled bells of the Abbey rang out their dirge, and Diana left on her long last journey, by hearse, through streets lined with more people, more flowers, back home to her family's Althorp estate in Northamptonshire.

All along the 77-mile route crowds hurled bouquets and single blooms at the hearse, like some grim battle of the flowers, and cried out their goodbyes until she arrived at Althorp.

There, at a short private service attended by the Spencer family, Prince Charles and her sons, they finally laid Diana to rest, wearing a formal, long-sleeved black dress she bought a few weeks earlier and had never worn, and with a rosary given to her by Mother Teresa of Calcutta.

Her simple grave is on a beautiful, tree-filled and newly-consecrated island on an ornamental lake called The Oval – a place Diana loved since she was a girl and where she and her sisters and sons had planted oaks for future generations to see and enjoy.

It was chosen rather than the traditional Spencer burial place – the family chapel in the parish church of St Mary the Virgin – so that sightseers would be deterred from laying constant siege to the quiet village of Great Brington.

And so, as Earl Spencer said, 'the grave can be properly looked after by the family and visited in privacy by her sons'.

'A wonderful place', said former Spencer housekeeper Betty Andrew, now 76. 'I used to go there in the early mornings to gather greenery to go with all the flowers in the house. It's beautiful and quiet and peaceful. A perfect place for Diana.'

By the evening of that achingly sad day she was at rest there, away from the spotlights and the headlines, the flashguns and the limelight in which she'd lived most of her cruelly short life.

Away from the rumours, the smears, the lies. Away from the agonies and anxieties that had plagued her.

She lies there now, alone on her own isolated and tranquil island, where no cares or concerns can reach her, where nothing and no-one can touch her.

The people's princess is the sleeping princess. In peace. At last.

Above: Diana's final resting place at Althorp – an island, away from the prying lenses of the Press.

Epitaph

"My sister – the unique, the complex, the extraordinary and irreplaceable Diana…"

"Diana was the very essence of compassion, of duty, of style, of beauty. All over the world, she was a symbol of selfless humanity. All over the world, a standard-bearer for the rights of the truly downtrodden, a very British girl who transcended nationality. Someone with a natural nobility who was classless and who proved in the last year that she needed no royal title to continue to generate her particular brand of magic."

Earl Spencer, from his funeral address,
Westminster Abbey, London, September 6th, 1997

Picture credits

The publishers would like to thank the following for their help in providing photographs for this book.

Alpha, London: 12-13, 14 top left and bottom right, 15, 17 bottom right, 18 bottom left, 19 top left and bottom, 32 bottom, top right, 37 top right, 38 inset top left, 40 top left, 41 top left and top right, 43 upper and lower right, 44 top, 45 bottom left, 47 top left, 49 top and bottom, 66, 67 top left and bottom left, 72-73, 75, 78 bottom right, 82 bottom left and right, 86 bottom left, 87, 88 top centre and bottom left, 90 right, 95 middle (Dave Chancellor), 101 bottom right,114 top right, 116 top left; **BBC:** 60-61 top centre; **Dave Benett:** 95 bottom right; **Camera Press:** 14 top right, 24, 28-9 (Lichfield), 30 bottom left, 35 (Lichfield), 55 (Snowdon), 68 top and bottom left, 76 top left, 84 all pictures, 85 all pictures, 90 bottom left, 92 top right, 95 bottom left, 101 left, 102, 139 (Patrick Demarchelier); **Eastern Counties Newspapers:** 18 top; **Fox/Central Press:** 22 top, 23;**The Independent:** 132 bottom (Brian Harris); **Julian Herbert:** 43 lower left; **Mirror Group Newspapers:** 6, 7 (Kent Gavin),17 left and top right, 18 bottom right and inset bottom centre, 20 bottom right, 21 left, 25 top left, centre left and bottom left, 27, 31 top, 32 top right, 33, 34 top, centre and bottom, 37 bottom, 38 top right and bottom, 39, 42 bottom centre, 43 top left, 45 right, 47 top right, bottom left and bottom right, 48 (Kent Gavin), 50, 51, 52 (Kent Gavin), 53, 54 (left), 54 right (Kent Gavin), 56, 58-59 (Kent Gavin), 60 inset top left, 61 right, 62, 63, 64 top, centre and bottom, 67 right, 72 inset, 74 inset top left and top right, 77, 78 top left (Kent Gavin) bottom left (Kent Gavin), 79 (Kent Gavin), 80, 81, 83, 86 inset top left (Kent Gavin), 89 (Kent Gavin), 91 (Kent Gavin), 92 bottom (Kent Gavin), 93, 94 (Kent Gavin), 96 inset top left and right, 97, 98-100 all pictures (Kent Gavin), 103-109 (Kent Gavin), 114 inset top left and bottom, 115 top left and bottom left, 121 inset, 124-125; **Portman Press:** 20 bottom left; **Press Association:** 12 inset top left,16, 19 top right, 20 centre right, 110-111, 115 top right and inset bottom right, 116 bottom left, 117 left, 118 top left and bottom left, 119 top right and middle and bottom left, 120; **Press Association Rota Photographers:** 128-131, 132 top pictures, 133-137; **Rex Features:** 5, 20 top left and top right, 21 right, 22 bottom, 25 right, 26 left and right, 30-31 centre bottom, 37 top left, 42 top and bottom right, 46 top right, 57, 58 inset, 60 bottom, 61 left, 68 bottom right, 69 top, 74 right, 76 right, 117 top right (Peter Heimsath) and bottom right, 118-119 top, 122 right, 123 top; **Reuters:** 116 right, 118 bottom right, 119 botom right; **Solent News Agency:** 36; **Syndication International:** 28 inset, 30 top, 32 top left, 40 top right (Kent Gavin), 40 bottom, 41 bottom, 44 bottom, 45 top left; **Universal Pictures International:** 71; Steve Wood: 95 top middle

Every effort has been made to contact copyright holders in cases where ownership is not clear.

Princess Diana's Charities

United Kingdom

**The Diana, Princess of Wales
Memorial Fund**
Kensington Palace
London W8 4PU

The British Red Cross*
Anti-Personnel Land Mines Campaign
No 9 Grosvenor Crescent
London SW1X 7EJ
*Ceased to be official patron in 1996

Centrepoint Soho
Bewlay House
2 Swallow Place
London W1R 7AA

English National Ballet
Markova House
39 Jay Mews
London SW7 2EF

The Leprosy Mission
Goldhay Way
Orton Goldhay
Peterborough PE2 5GZ

National Aids Trust
Princess Diana Fund
New City Cloisters
188-196 Old Street
London EC1V 9FR

Royal Marsden NHS Trust
Fulham Rd
London SW3 6JJ

**Great Ormond St Hospital
for Children NHS Trust**
Great Ormond St
London WC1N 3JH

United States

American Red Cross
17th and D Streets NW
Washington, D.C. 20006